Cleeve Common
and the
North Cotswolds

Including walks over Cleeve Common and the neighbourhood

with a short exploration of the North Cotswolds

John V. Garrett, 1993

To Maureen with love

Cotswold Ways

One comes across the strangest things in walks: ...
Old troughs, great stone cisterns bishops might have blessed
Ceremonially, and worthy mounting stones;
Black timber in red brick, queerly placed
Where hill stone was looked for —

Ivor Gurney

Contents

ACKNOWLEDGEMENTS

The publishers and author would like to express their appreciation to the Cheltenham Art
Gallery and Museums Service for permission to reproduce a detail from the eighteenth-century
painting of Dixton Manor in the Cheltenham Art Gallery, to the Ministry of Defence for
permission to reproduce their RAF aerial photograph of Cleeve Common (Crown copyright
reserved), to Richard Mabey for permission to use the extract from his book *The Common Ground*
at the heading of chapter two and to Oxford University Press for permission to use an extract
from the *Collected Poems of Ivor Gurney* edited by P. J. Kavanagh (OUP 1982).
The photographs, with the exception of the aerial photograph and those copied from *From a
Cotswold Height* and one of the sheep wash in use, are by the author.

CLEEVE COMMON AND THE NORTH COTSWOLDS

First published by Thornhill Press Ltd (1993)
3 Fountain Way, Parkend, Forest of Dean, Glos.

© John V. Garrett

Typeset by Carnegie Publishing Ltd., Preston
Printed in the UK by The Cromwell Press, Melksham, Wilts

ISBN 0 946328 46 3

Introduction

ABRIEF GLANCE at the local books section of any bookseller in Cheltenham, Gloucester or the neighbouring towns will show a plethora of books with 'Cotswold' in their title. What then is the excuse for the appearance of yet another? The explanation lies in the fact that this is an unusual book. In 1919 a book by the father of the present writer appeared entitled *From a Cotswold Height*, a description of Cleeve Hill and its neighbourhood near Cheltenham. It enjoyed a modest success. The present writer on returning to Cleeve Hill on retirement was surprised to find it still well known and well thought of by residents in the area. It is in fact very readable today, of far more relevance it may be thought, than the much better known *Cotswold Village* by J. Arthur Gibbs, which seems now to describe an impossibly Arcadian world.

Long out of print *From a Cotswold Height* was difficult to obtain until a reprint was organised by David Aldred, a local resident, and published by Alan Sutton Publishing Ltd in 1988. This has now again been reprinted.

This local interest together with the undoubted attractiveness of the area led the present writer to think that a modern version based on his knowledge of the area, bringing the information up to date, mentioning the changes that had occurred and including walks more suitable for today which he had found specially interesting on account of scenery or history, might be of value.

This book takes a small area of the Cotswolds north-east of Cheltenham, particularly around Cleeve Hill, and describes it in some detail. The first chapter describes the basic features of the area and mentions the changes that have occurred in it over the last seventy years particularly those due to increased population and alterations in agricultural practice. Other chapters describe the great expanse of Cleeve Common, and walks over it, around the hill and to other places in the vicinity. Finally, following the plan of the old book, there is a description of a drive in the north Cotswolds to take in some of the interesting and historic places there. Some of the descriptions of the plants and places are rather more detailed than is usual in books of a general nature but this is a deliberate feature in the belief that many readers would like to know more about the places they visit. However in order to preserve sites from interference no details of the positions of the rarer or more easily disturbed wildlife features are given. All visitors should observe the Country Code and, especially when on Cleeve Common, keep their dogs under control.

The walks described can be followed on the Ordnance Survey's 2½ inches to 1 mile (1/25,000) *Pathfinder* maps. Sheets 1042, 1066, 1067 cover most of the area described. Many of the paths are obvious enough not to need the maps but they will enhance the interest. The area is also covered by *Landranger* (1/50,000) sheets 150 and 163 and the inch to 1 mile Tourist Map 8 of the Cotswolds.

1

Most of the paths have been well waymarked by the County Rights of Way department or the Cotswold Voluntary Wardens. A yellow arrow marks footpaths, the Cotswold Way has a yellow arrow with a white dot. Bridle ways have a blue arrow. The Wychavon Way has a W sign.

The large map in the book is reproduced from the one in *From a Cotswold Height* partly brought up to date with corrections and additions of major features. I am indebted to Michael Hickey for the botanical drawings of grasses.

Very many people have contributed to the author's knowledge of the region. Among them are Ted Fryer, John Milner, David Aldred, Michael Gilder, Jennifer Jackson, Adrian Lawson, George Pockett, Michael Wilkinson, Susan Dudley-Smith, Mr and Mrs Barrett, John Yiend, the late Sonia Holland, the late Tom Denley, the late T. F. Evans and the staffs of Cheltenham Public Library and Gloucester Library and Gloucestershire Record Office. The author could not have written this book without their help but takes all responsibility for facts and opinions. Information from the records of the Board of Conservators of Cleeve Common was obtained when the author was a member of that body and is included with their permission.

Chapter One

An outline of the Cotswold scene and changes in it over the last seventy years

[The Cotswolds are] also linked to twentieth-century perceptions as a place where time has stood still, and where it is still possible to re-establish age-old links between nature and humanity. This concept was comparatively new ... in the 1920s: today, with growing awareness about environmental problems, it is widespread and this is one of the reasons why the Cotswolds is such a highly valued landscape, both nationally and internationally.

The Cotswold Landscape
Countryside Commission 1990.

PROPERLY SPEAKING Cotswold refers only to the limestone hills extending from the western scarp towards the Thames valley in the east by a gentle dip slope, and lying in the area between the Bath Avon and the Warwickshire Avon rivers, with the villages at the foot of the scarp. However, in recent years, as the name became known as an attractive tourist area, it has been expanded conveniently but incorrectly, to much of the upper and eastern part of the Vales of Gloucester and of Evesham.

The area with which this book deals is the North Cotswolds north and east of Cheltenham, and extends by visits to the outlying limestone hills and to the north east where the country is over the county border in Oxfordshire.

Modern place-name scholarship, taking its clues from the earliest written form of the name, considers that Cotswold, first appearing written as Codeswalt, is derived from the Saxon personal name Cod, and wald, a forest—Cod's forest. Later wald became Wold—open rolling hills. This derivation has replaced the previously favoured one that Cots meant sheep cotes or pens.

The hills are part of the great limestone belt of Jurassic age that extends from the Dorset coast to Yorkshire. Cleeve Hill is the highest part of this range rising to 1,083 feet or 330 metres. In our area the rocks are composed of oolitic limestone lying on the Lias clay which covers the Vale. The name oolite is given because of the fine-grained appearance like fish roe, which can be seen in most rock samples from the area. The limestone was laid down by deposition from a warm shallow sea, 150–200 million years ago, at the time the Atlantic Ocean was forming. At first the limestone hills extended much further towards the west

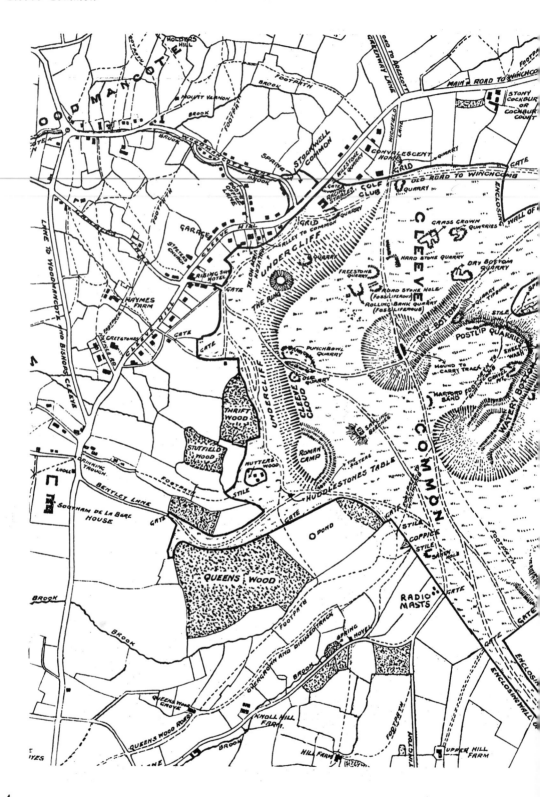

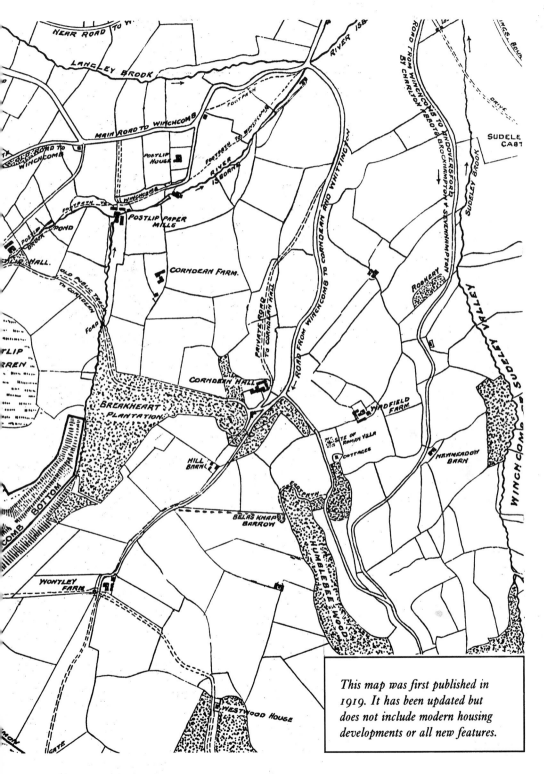

This map was first published in 1919. It has been updated but does not include modern housing developments or all new features.

but have gradually been eroded back so that now only isolated outliers capped with harder rock are left in what is now the Vale of Severn.

In many places in our area the hills rise by a steep scarp from the Vale and this forms an impressive sight especially when seen in the afternoon sun from the Cheltenham Racecourse area. This cliff forms Cleeve Cloud, which has been quarried for building stone for centuries up to recent times.

At the top of the hills is a nearly flat plateau of small extent and then the slope dips toward the east. This means that almost all the Cotswold streams flow

Air photo. Cleeve Common on 17 August 1947 from 13,950 ft.

eastward towards the Thames valley. The four main streams are, from north to south, the Evenlode, the Windrush, the Coln and the Churn and their tributaries. Only a few short streams flow west or north to join the Severn or Avon. Parts of the valleys of the eastward flowing streams are wooded and make up a characteristic feature of the Cotswold scene.

The colour of the stone varies being more brown or yellow towards the north where the amount of iron is greater, and pale grey towards the south. In places it contains many fossils but where it is free of them it makes excellent building stone which enabled the local people to create the Cotswold stone villages so much appreciated today. The appearance of the old houses is enhanced by being roofed with stone tiles which came from special quarries. The other feature of the Cotswold scene, the stone walls, are made of stone of lower quality often picked off the fields, and most were built after the enclosure of the wolds in the eighteenth and nineteenth centuries. Old photographs show the open treeless aspect of the wolds now less obvious with plantations and the growth of scrub trees especially along roadsides. Unfortunately the field walls, being of stone which easily shatters in frost, are in many places suffering decay.

These features, the open landscape, the hills and wooded valleys, the stone villages, the stone walled fields are those that give the 'diversity in unity' which makes the district so attractive. The scene that I think of as epitomising these features is one in which a yellow track climbs gently through yellowish grassland, sprinkled with white and yellow flowers, towards a blue sky with a stone barn on the skyline, and a beech wood bounded by a grey stone wall at its side. Such scenes are often to be found in the area covered by this book.

The hills, apart from the valleys, had probably been cleared of wood by the Bronze Age and from that time were used for pasturing large numbers of sheep and cattle. Sheep pasturage continued into the Middle Ages and wool was the chief product of the area. Northleach, Chipping Campden, and Witney became great wool centres where the wool was collected for export. The abbeys of Gloucester and Winchcombe especially had great flocks on the hills. The woolmen accumulated great wealth and used some of it to build the great wool churches that are admired today. By the eighteenth century however this trade had declined and more land was converted to arable though sheep were still numerous. In the vale at the foot of the scarp dairy farming and fruit growing were dominant. Most of the orchards were of cider apples.

My father's book of 1919 was written from notes made between 1910 and 1918 and describes an agricultural country. It was however inevitable that a place like Bishop's Cleeve, so near to Cheltenham, would soon change. The start of this was described in a very prescient way in that book—'a greater modernity due to touch with the fashionable town that lies but three miles away, shows its influence in the sons and daughters who have lived there and have returned, or who go to and fro daily by bicycle or train bringing back with them innovations of dress and ideas, manners and speech.'

The development of Smith's Industries since 1940 caused a tenfold increase in the population of Bishop's Cleeve from 615 in 1921 to 6,126 in 1981 and an almost entire re-building of the village centre. In the same way Southam rose

7

from 220 people to 684 and many of the old cottages were demolished as not reaching acceptable standards. In Woodmancote perhaps the change in land use is best seen in the almost complete disappearance of orchards. The map of 1923 shows 110 acres of them in that parish. Their pleasant appearance in spring is well described in the old book and older residents remember the rows of white-washed trunks in winter.

The mechanisation of farming with the purchase of expensive machinery, and the reduction of labour this achieves, has meant the disappearance of many small farms with a concentration into larger units. Since many times as much work can be done by machines as by the old methods this has meant a migration of farm workers from the countryside. In the 1930s, for example, there were at least six small dairy herds in the part of the vale below Cleeve Hill each of a size that could be milked by hand. These have all disappeared. Taken with the disappearance of horses from farms and the replacement of hay making by silage making, this has meant a great loss in the variety of country scenes compared with fifty years ago. For instance, one old resident of Cleeve Hill described to me the wagons laden with stone descending the steep lanes. Drawn by great cart horses their speed was checked by locking one wheel with an iron slipper drag which struck sparks from the stones in the road.

Change is inevitable and although you may look over a gate into a deserted farmyard so recently the scene of activity, and regret that its buildings are to be converted into housing or business units, this is surely better than that it should be demolished or left to decay. In this way at least the characteristic buildings can be saved. The new public uses for the great barns at Bishop's Cleeve and Southam are good examples of new uses for old buildings enabling them to continue to play an important part in the villages where they have stood for centuries.

Cotswold villages in the hills are now as likely to be inhabited by retired professional people or by long-distance commuters as by those working locally. This has meant that there are few houses affordable by the young. The consequence has often been a closing of the village school and village shop, and more recently even of the village inn. These changes have meant a collapse of the old style of village life to the regret of the few original villagers left.

Not all is for the worse however. The spread of owner occupancy has lead to an improvement in housing quality. In a few places you may find a village where for various reasons this has not yet happened and it looks much as one remembers the villages of pre-war days. The greater ease of private transport has been the chief cause of these changes, but it also enables local communities to take part in a wider range of activities.

Modern farming changes have greatly altered the countryside scene. Following the government's encouragement to convert more land from pasture to arable, many of the grasslands of the Cotswolds were ploughed up in the war and later. This change is recorded in the land use maps of the 1930s and 1960s. The supplement to the *Gloucestershire Flora* of 1986 records that six major areas of downland rough grazing had been lost since the survey for the earlier flora was published in 1948. The arable has usually been planted to cereals, in the

Cotswolds often barley, and large areas look like a monoculture of that crop, which again means there is less variety of scene.

An alteration in farming practice contributing greatly to changes in the scenery is the decline in grazing. This is particularly noticeable on the scarp slopes following the reduction in the number of dairy herds and active sheep rearing. The increase in 'pony paddocks' does not compensate for this. Together with the reduction in rabbit numbers following the myxomatosis epidemic of the 1950s, the decrease in grazing has meant an increase in growth of coarse grasses and scrub. This is well shown in the two pictures of the slopes of Nottingham Hill taken from the same spot on Cleeve Hill in about 1918 and 1990.

The changes brought about by these alterations in farming practice were intensified by the use of chemical pesticides and herbicides to control insects and weeds considered pests. Justified at the time by the arguments for greater food production and efficient farm-ing, they resulted in intensive

Top: Nottingham Hill from Cleeve Common before 1919.

Below: The same view in 1990.

farming with a further inevitable loss of variety. Though these changes are greatest in the intensively cultivated area of East Anglia, they have occurred in the Cotswolds and Vale. The effects can be seen particularly in the changes in birds and flowers.

Looking at the descriptions of bird life in Gloucestershire early in this century it seems that species and flocks were recorded in numbers which are not seen now. My father recorded, admittedly at a guess, a flock of rooks and starlings 2,000 strong at a small copse near Sudeley, which is still recognisable (Wadfield Grove) and still used by rooks, though now scarcely more than twenty are likely to be seen there.

The Wold scene 1993. Sudeley Hill Barn, early spring.

His evening walk from Belas Knap was enlivened by seeing and hearing a nightjar which at that time was fairly common in Cotswold woods. Now you are not likely to see this species outside the Forest of Dean.

Though the wild area on the slopes of Nottingham Hill above Woodmancote mentioned by him still exists with its bracken and brambles you will not see a shrike there. That species is now extinct in Britain and much diminished throughout Europe.

A familiar bird of open country is the lapwing with its wheeling flight and shrill cry. Mellersh, in his *Treatise on the Birds of Gloucestershire* of 1902, reports a flock of 10,000 of these birds which darkened the sky over Cleeve Common. It must be some time since such numbers were seen anywhere.

A common bird of the fields in pre-war days was the grey partridge, and a covey of a dozen birds could often be seen in the stubble. Today they are uncommon and have been affected, like others, by the scarcity of their insect food and by the prevalence of autumn ploughing, the fields not being left in stubble over the winter.

Although not all these declines in bird numbers can be attributed to changes in farming methods, some already being on the way before the new agricultural revolution, and others being affected by changes overseas, there is little doubt that the country today has fewer bird numbers than seventy years ago.

Plants too have been affected. The loss of grassland reported in the new *Gloucestershire Flora* has already been mentioned, and the same book states that fifty-six native species of plants have probably become extinct in the county since 1948. As well as changes in grassland and arable farming there has also been the decline in woodland coppicing and the substitution of conifers for hardwoods in some woodlands. This has meant that many woodland species have apparently suffered a decline as the canopy has not been removed at about ten-year intervals as was the case when coppicing was done. Such a wood is Thrift Wood on Cleeve Hill where my father noted in 1912 plants of Solomon's seal and autumn crocus which do not seem to be there now.

If in the last fifty years the balance of government intervention has been decisively tipped towards the promotion of food production and profitable farming, it is beginning to be realised that encouragement of conservation measures is now necessary. A voluntary advice group, the Farming and Wildlife Advice Group (FWAG) has been set up to give advice about wildlife matters to farmers requesting it.

The debate about the de-intensification of farming is linked with the realisation that European Community agricultural policy has resulted in the accumulation of vast stocks of foodstuffs saleable only at subsidised prices. This has led to the recent introduction, among other measures, of the 'set aside' policy in which a subsidy is paid for not growing crops on a proportion of the land. Weeds and scrub are to be controlled only by mowing and cultivation. Understandably this is considered practically immoral by many farmers and its effect on the countryside has yet to be seen. A development of this is the Environmentally Sensitive Areas scheme which is likely to be applied to part of the Cotswolds before long. This will enable farmers to apply for grants towards the cost of preserving or restoring unimproved grassland and for the repair of dry stone walls. In this way the characteristic features of the traditional landscape may be maintained.

Another aspect of farming policy is the promotion of new crops such as linseed and sunflowers which provide new sights in the countryside. The most dramatic of these, though it is not new, is the growing of oil seed rape which produces fields of bright yellow in early summer.

The legal framework of modern countryside policy started with the National Parks and Access to the Countryside Act of 1949. This enabled National Parks and Areas of Outstanding Natural Beauty (AONBs) to be designated and following it the Cotswolds were designated an AONB in 1966. This gives some, but not an absolute, protection to the traditional features of the area. Under this Act and under the Wildlife and Countryside Act of 1981 areas of particular interest could be designated Sites of Special Scientific Interest (SSSIs). Most of Cleeve Common became such an area in 1974. The Act requires any operation which is likely to damage the special features of such an area to be notified to the Nature Conservancy, now English Nature, which cannot prevent, but can delay its being carried out, during which time alternative procedures may be arranged.

The area between the boundary of Cheltenham's built-up area and Southam and Bishop's Cleeve has been given Green Belt status which has kept that area free of building development which would otherwise certainly have happened.

Development has proceeded in other areas and the planning process has not always been successful in preventing undesirable intrusions into the landscape, as can be seen in the view from Cleeve Hill where the light-coloured roofs of industrial buildings intrude into the rural scene. The fact that, at least until recently, farm buildings did not require planning consent, has meant that some very incongruous buildings have found their way into the Cotswold scene.

The decline of the old stone quarry industry has meant that, although so–called traditional materials are usually stipulated for new domestic buildings in the AONB, they are now usually made of crushed and reconstituted stone which does not have quite the appearance of the old stone blocks. Especially the new types of roof tiles are of different character from the old stone slates in that they do not encourage the growth of lichens and weather differently, if at all. Nevertheless the use of these modern labour-saving materials has enabled something of the traditional regional character to be retained.

All the factors mentioned here, and others, have meant that the Cotswolds have seen more changes in the last fifty years than for centuries before. The superficial traveller by car may feel that the Cotswolds are still an unspoilt area retaining their special character, but as we have seen there have been many changes in detail.

However, fortunately some things have not changed. It is still possible to get a great sense of freedom walking over Cleeve Common and the jackdaws still wheel over the cliffs of Cleeve Cloud. The valleys and villages in the hills are still pleasant to explore especially on foot, and the area is a most attractive one for those who know what to look for. The following chapters will try to describe it and help in its appreciation. The next fifty years will no doubt see even greater changes but fortunately there is now a greater understanding of the needs of the countryside as a whole. Though there cannot be a return to the ways of the past we must create an environment which is pleasant to live in without destroying the source of that pleasure.

Chapter Two

Cleeve Hill and its Common

But the fact is we do not want the natural world preserved as a museum piece. We want the opportunity to experience it face to face, with its qualities of wildness and renewal intact. We want, all of us, to hang on to favourite places and familiar creatures, and to the uniquely private network of meaning and association which attaches to them.

R. Mabey, *The Common Ground* (1980).

THE EXTENT of Cleeve Hill Common is just over 1,000 acres (approximately 405 hectares) and its periphery is about ten miles round. The fact that it forms a very special piece of country should be clear to anyone who walks up the gentle slope to the top of the track rising from the golf clubhouse. The vast expanse of open country stretching away nearly one and a half miles to the radio masts on the horizon and beyond, the intriguing valleys with their old quarries and tracks in the foreground, the scarp with its views across the great vale nearer at hand, all contribute to a memorable scene. It is remarkable to think that, in essentials, this landscape today is probably not much different from what it would have been 2,500 years ago when Bronze Age people had cleared the area of trees and begun to use it for their sheep and cattle. How has this area survived as open land when all around has been enclosed? The answer lies partly in geology and partly in the history of land use.

As we have seen the geology of the area is that of the oolitic limestone scarp and the dip country to the east. Many of the slopes are too steep for cultivation and the soil in many places is thin. The best use of such an area is for pasture and it has been used for that purpose since Bronze Age times.

History

The detailed history of Cleeve Common has recently been well written by David Aldred, (*Cleeve Hill, The History of the Common and its People*, Alan Sutton, 1990) and only a brief outline will be given here.

The area of Cleeve Common was included in the Anglo-Saxon charter which defined the estate which was to become the parish of Bishop's Cleeve and was allocated to the Bishop of Worcester. The common was considered as part of the waste, that is to say uncultivated land, of the manor. This ensured that the inhabitants of Bishop's Cleeve and the neighbouring hamlets of Southam and Woodmancote had the right to graze their sheep and cattle on it in the summer and it was clearly of great value to them. Over 1,000 sheep are reported to have

View of Cleeve Cloud scarp from Southam.

grazed it in medieval times and disputes between the villages are recorded. Later the right to graze was limited to people who had enough land in the vale to support the same number of animals in winter as they grazed on the Common in summer, but this rule was often broken.

By the nineteenth century enclosure of open land for improving agriculture was in full swing. Prestbury had been enclosed in 1732, Gotherington in 1808 including the top of Nottingham Hill, previously open common. Bishop's Cleeve enclosure was in 1847 but Cleeve Common was not included. In the vestry of Bishop's Cleeve church are the minutes of the meeting at which the commoners decided against enclosure.

Lord Ellenborough of Southam, the lord of the manor, had sent a letter to the churchwardens about enclosure and at a meeting held on 7 January 1848 the villagers with rights on the Common voted on a proposal that the hill should be enclosed. Ten voted in favour of enclosure and thirty against. In this way the open common was saved for posterity, otherwise it might have become much as the top of Nottingham Hill is today. We therefore owe its continued existence as an open common to those thirty villagers of Bishop's Cleeve of 1848.

The air photograph shows the relationship of the Common to surrounding areas. The distinction between the large areas of the higher ground enclosed under Enclosure Acts and the smaller fields of earlier enclosures is well seen.

However, problems were not over with the rejection of the enclosure scheme. For a number of years there had been arguments over the use of the Common by people from Cheltenham and elsewhere who exercised their horses there and had started a race meeting, to the detriment of the sheep graziers. This led to many conflicts and eventually a scheme of management was set up under a special Act of Parliament in 1890 with the establishment of a Board of

*The Lonely Road.
The White Way at
Barnard's Cross.*

Conservators which is still in existence. The members of the board are drawn from the inhabitants of the parishes of Bishop's Cleeve, Southam and Wood-mancote with three members representing Cheltenham, since the borough was to provide £50 a year towards the expenses of management in return for the privilege of its inhabitants being able ride and walk on the Common. In recent years co-opted members have been added.

Present management

Conflicts, however, continue and are not helped by misunderstandings of the nature of common land and its use. Too often the term 'common' is thought of as meaning public ownership of an area over which the public have the right to do whatever they wish. A moment's thought should show that such an anarchic idea cannot be right. In law 'common' land is still owned by someone, even if it is a local authority,or, as in the case of Cleeve, the lord of the manor. It still has to be managed and protected from misuse by a set of rules.

In the case of Cleeve, under the 1890 Act all management is done by the Board of Conservators which has drawn up a set of bye-laws for the regulation of the Common. The board has power to issue licences for specific activities on the Common, for which it may charge an annual fee. The wording of the bye-laws may seem to reflect the ideas and needs of the 1890s rather than those of the 1990s, but the most important controls are included in modern general legislation.

The Common is registered under the Commons Registration Act of 1965 with twenty-three registered land holdings with grazing rights. Even if the

Old Postlip Quarries and Tracks.

View near Postlip Gate.

owners of some of these no longer exercise their rights, grazing is still actively carried out and is an essential part of the management of the Common.

Pressure from other uses has increased greatly in the last 100 years. A golf club was established in 1890 and play on the Common started the following year. The first course was laid out on the lower slopes and suited the golfers of that time. Since then several successive courses have been laid out following changes in playing techniques, and there is now a 6,411-yards par-72 course over about half of the Common. Racehorse training has continued and the gallops on the flat part of the Common near the radio masts and on West Down are actively used. The Common is also an excellent place for ordinary riders to exercise their horses. Both these activities are regulated by the Board which requires licences to be taken out for them.

There are also the usual activities of rambling, kite flying and dog exercising by local people as well as rock climbing and orienteering by people from a wider area. After a snowfall the slopes above the main road may be black with people enjoying tobogganing and even skiing. The Common is a valuable educational resource for schools which use it for field study and for cadet force exercises.

Landscape and geology

Cleeve Common is the largest area of unimproved limestone grassland in Glouces-tershire and one of the largest areas in the South West. This means that it has never been ploughed or systematically treated with fertilisers. It is said that 50 per cent of the surviving unimproved Jurassic limestone grassland in England and Wales is in the Cotswolds, and Cleeve Common contains about a third of that. Many areas of Cotswold grassland have been ploughed up and improved in the last forty-five years, as we have seen in the previous chapter. The importance of Cleeve as one of the few places where the natural characteristics of such land and its great variety of plant species have survived is therefore clear. This botanical importance, together with its geological features, was recognised by its designation as a Site of Special Scientific Interest in 1974 under the 1949 National Parks and Access to the Countryside Act. This was confirmed under the Wildlife and Countryside Act of 1981 and the site is considered of Grade 1 importance. As we have seen this gives a measure of protection against unauthorised change. Under the Wildlife and Countryside Act all birds and their nests are protected except game and pest species. The Board of Conservators gives licences for catching rabbits on the Common but all other animals are protected. Since 1991 adders have been protected under the 1981 Act.

Cleeve Common consists of three main parts. These are the scarp slope and undercliff, the plateau at the top, prolonged south eastwards into the long strip of West Down, and the dip slope on the eastern side with its three steep-sided valleys. These valleys are, from north to south, Dry Bottom which has no water in it on the Common, Watery Bottom with several springs which run down into a pool made in 1897 to provide water for a stone sheep wash just below, and Padcombe Bottom, also without a spring on the Common.

Several parts of the Common have been given distinctive names by local people. The Knolls is the area around the single beech at the top of the slope above the Camp. Middle Hill is between Watery and Dry Bottoms. The name North Hill can be given to the part north of Dry Bottom. The Slips is the area affected by landslip just below the houses of Nutterswood, now planted with trees, and Watch House is the high area bordering Postlip Warren. The old quarries have their own names, most of which are shown on the map in this book.

The single beech.

The slopes of Watery Bottom—sheep coming to drink.s

The rocks, as partly explained earlier, are of the oolitic limestone of the Inferior or Lower Oolite series lying on the Upper Lias clay. This junction of pervious limestone with impervious clay results in a springline where the water, having percolated through the limestone, comes to the surface, as is seen in the springs of Spring Lane and above Nutterswood on the west side and in Watery Bottom on the east. As well as the limestone an important feature is the Harford Sands. These form a thin layer near the top of the Common in several places and on the upper south-east slopes of Watery Bottom. Unlike the rest of the Common they have a faintly acid reaction, the calcium having been leached out, and this has the interesting effect of enabling acid-loving plants (calcifuge) to grow close to those preferring alkaline soil (calcicole species).

Where the limestone is thickest and free of large fossils, it forms a freestone which could be cut in any plane, and made it a valuable building stone. It was used for centuries for churches and other buildings in the neighbourhood, such as Bishop's Cleeve church. In more modern times—for extraction of stone was carried out to about 1940—it was still used for buildings. It is recorded that All Saints Church, Cheltenham, was built at least partly from Cleeve Hill stone (Verey, *Buildings of Gloucestershire*, vol. 2) and the large country house, Besford Court near Pershore, was built with it in 1912. The stone for this came from Arthur Yiend's quarries on the hill. He lived at Glendale, Post Office Lane, Cleeve Hill, and built the stone houses along that road and Besford Road.

In a more humble way the Harford Sands also had uses. An early geology book on the Cheltenham area (Richardson, 1904, p. 99) quotes evidence that strings of pack-donkeys took the sand to the Staffordshire potteries where it was mixed with clay to make a suitable slip. Another use was as polishing sand for the marble sculpture works in Cheltenham.

Some of the quarries, particularly the one known as Rolling Bank near the eighteenth tee of the golf course, are known to be rich in fossils. This quarry is noted for the fossils of a snail-like creature called *Bourgetia*, and for a band of very hard limestone known as the Phillipsiana beds, found nowhere else in Britain. The slopes of Postlip Warren, not on the Common but just over the wall to the east, are important to geologists as showing characteristic 'ridge and trough' features where blocks of limestone have slipped downwards over the clay towards the north.

The open landscape of the Common was created by prehistoric man for pasturing his animals, and its preservation depends on continued grazing at a high level of intensity. Traditionally the Common was open for grazing from 25 April to 30 November. The opening date was sometimes delayed if it was considered there was not enough grass. In the 1980s sheep were often not put on the Common until after the first compulsory dipping in June or July. In the years since the Second World War changes in grazing have meant that the flora of the Common has changed. This is not peculiar to Cleeve but is a problem in many other similar places, particularly the commons of the Gloucestershire Cotswolds.

Grazing pressure has decreased owing to a number of factors. These include the shorter time sheep now often spend on the Common in summer, and the smaller number of farmers who are interested in putting their sheep on the hill, although they have grazing rights. Also to the cessation of grazing by cattle and horses and by the reduction in number of rabbits due to the myxomatosis epidemic which first appeared in the 1950s. Records of the Board of Conservators show that appreciable numbers of cattle and horses used to be kept on the Common. For instance, the stock list for 1946 shows 546 sheep, 347 lambs, 64 cattle and 19 horses on the Common that year. The last horses were recorded in 1958 and the cattle ceased in the late 1960s or early 1970s as the method of cattle-rearing altered, the beasts being sold off the farm at an earlier age.

These changes have resulted in the growth of scrub woodland in some places at the edges of the Common, and to a great increase in the coarse tor grass (*Brachypodium*) which is not eaten by most breeds of sheep when they can get enough to eat from the finer grasses. This grass was kept down by the cattle and horses. There has also been a great spread of gorse which is confirmed by air photographs of the Common which have been taken at intervals from 1946. These show that the gorse has spread particularly since the late 1960s. Previously parts of the Common used to be burnt in early springtime. The effect of this on the tor grass is controversial but it may have helped to control the gorse. This, though it may look marvellous in spring when it is in bloom, has spread so much as to reduce the area of grazing and produces impenetrable thickets of thorny bushes. Its control is an expensive and labour-intensive process. A small amount is used for making jumps for the racecourse.

From 1821 a man was employed to look after the sheep on the Common and ensure that only the animals of common-rights holders were allowed there. He had the name of Haywarden. It is recorded that in 1912 he was paid £1 a week with an extra one shilling a week for his dog's keep. At this time the Board's income was probably no more than £150 a year. In the late twentieth century the work was done by members of local families, notably the Hamletts and Denleys. The last Tom Denley retired in 1988.

At the time of writing the work of wardening the Common is shared between three part-timers. These are a general or bye-law warden who exercises general supervision, a shepherd who looks after the sheep in summer and autumn, and a gallops warden who maintains the race horse gallops and assists riders from September to May.

On the ancient tracks and routes

The great Common is crossed by many obvious tracks, now mostly grass grown. The study of them is a fascinating subject and is well covered in Aldred's book on the history of Cleeve Hill. Only an outline account of those of particular interest to the present-day walker is given here. Some are clearly quarry tracks going to the quarries overlooking Postlip which were once so busy. Others are of great antiquity. The most important of them is the one known as the White Way, not to be confused with other White Ways in Gloucestershire.

This comes up from the vale village of Gotherington, where it may be a continuation of a route coming from the north through the gap between the Dixton and Woolstone hills. The recognisable part of it starts on the Gotherington–Winchcombe road and ascends Nottingham Hill by a sunken holloway, a characteristic feature of an old road. It is probably the one mentioned as the 'Women's Way' in the boundaries of the Anglo-Saxon estate which became the parish of Bishop's Cleeve. It is described as going to Coca's Burh or camp. This

Sheep round-up.   is most likely to be the Iron Age camp on the top of Nottingham Hill. The name persists as Cockbury. In this area the way has the ancient name of Granna or Grinnell Lane and part of it is still the parish boundary. This track crosses Nottingham Hill top between stone walls, joins Bushcombe Lane, becomes known as Wickfield Lane, crosses the modern main road, and enters the Common by the golf clubhouse or Wickfield entrance. It crosses the Common, where it is known as the White Way, in a southerly direction and eventually leaves it at its furthest point, the end of West Down. Beyond this another short stretch of holloway can be found descending to the valley of West Wood and joining the road there. Its direction can be continued by small roads southwards towards the Roman settlement at Syreford or eastwards towards Stow on the Wold and Burford. On West Down it is crossed by a north-south track called today the Welsh Way, which comes from the area of Winchcombe and goes towards Syreford.

Fortunately for those who like to study old routes the road from Cheltenham to Winchcombe is one of the 100 routes all over England and Wales which John Ogilby mapped and published for Charles II as the first road atlas in 1675. It is shown as part of the road from Gloucester to Coventry and is mapped and described in some detail. The part that concerns us is the road between Prestbury and Winchcombe. The ascent of Cleeve Hill is shown beginning twelve miles from Gloucester after leaving Prestbury, and goes north-eastwards leaving a lane to Southam on the left. At the top further turnings to Southam and Swindon village are marked, one of them passing the 'Beacon' presumably at the highest point, or at the Camp. A turning to Burford is shown and the road continues as two unfenced routes over the pasture land of the Common. It meets a road from Cleeve, probably Stockwell Lane, and descends to the west of Postlip Hall, towards Winchcombe.

Today this road from Prestbury can be traced through Noverton, or by Mill Lane, and it is possible to find two or three routes up the hill. These could have been alternatives used according to local conditions. The most direct is the one past the group of houses known as Queenwood Grove, continuing up as a shallow holloway to meet a track now forming part of the Cotswold Way. This enters the Common at the point known as Wheeler's Gate. It then continues northwards to meet the White Way where it crosses the top of Dry Bottom on a low embankment. This meeting place is probably the place marked as Barnard's Cross on the first one-inch-to-one-mile map of Gloucestershire made by Isaac Taylor in 1777. It continues down Dry Bottom with the tower of Winchcombe church beckoning in the distance, to the boundary wall of Postlip Hall grounds. It then turns northwards and joins the track from Wickfield gate and the present golf house to descend to the main road.

The sheep sorting gate.

This route was the main road between Cheltenham and Winchcombe until the improved route avoiding the steepest part of the climb was made in 1792. This later road, now known as the 'Old Winchcombe Road', leaves the main road just above Southam, as Asleigh Lane, continues as a bridleway behind the houses up to Spring Lane, then behind the Rising Sun hotel and the youth hostel to join the extension of Stockwell Lane near Cleeve Lodge Stables. Old postcards show a well-worn track to the west of Cleeve Lodge stables, more in the direct line of the lane, unlike the present one to the east. The 1792 road runs northwards leaving the Common at the place where the field called Oat Piece encroaches onto it. It enters the Common again briefly before leaving it at the Postlip gate where, as stated above, it meets the ancient road to descend by a shady track to the main road. It was itself replaced by the modern line of road in 1823 with even easier gradients. There have therefore been three ways from Cheltenham to Winchcombe over the centuries, becoming successively easier if less direct.

It is of great interest that Ogilby shows a branch to Southam from near the top of the hill. This seems very likely to be the present Bentley Lane. This ascends the hill from nearly opposite the end of Southam Lane opposite the entrance of the Southam Delabere Hotel, passes through a gate which marks the boundary of the Common, and climbs along the edge of Queen's Wood. In

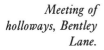

Meeting of holloways, Bentley Lane.

places there are four or five alternative, nearly parallel, deep holloways. This arrangement is often seen where an old route ascends a steep slope. When one way became impassable another beside it was started. Once open woodland, this area is now overgrown and a lonely and mysterious place. You walk up the deep channels climbing over fallen logs on the way. Of all the old trackways in the area it is to me the most evocative, and you can imagine early travellers toiling up the hill and horses and carts laden with stone from the quarries coming down.

Archaeological sites

The Common shows many other signs of habitation and use by ancient peoples. The largest is the promontory hillfort on the top of the scarp overlooking Nutterswood. This commands a marvellous view of the Vale and the valley of the Chelt above Cheltenham. It has two ditches and two banks enclosing an area bounded on the west by the cliffs of the scarp and quarries. It was originally larger but a significant part has been quarried away. When the golf course was built in 1891 a green was constructed just within the outer ditch. This remains in use and must be one of the most remarkable golf greens in the country. The fort is one of the chain of Iron Age camps extending all along the Cotswold scarp from the Bath Avon to Warwickshire.

The Ring is a small circular earthwork just above the youth hostel. It consists of a ditch and low mound. It also was altered during the construction of the golf course and became the eighteenth green of the first course. Near it is another small circular earthwork now practically enveloped in gorse. These structures may be of Iron Age date, but one cannot be sure about their use or date.

The area near Cleeve Lodge stables and the area of the beeches above the Rising Sun Lane entrance were the sites of excavations in the early 1900s. Workmen in the gravel pit close to King's Beeches reported finding bones, and when an excavation was carried out a number of pits with human and animal bones were found, suggesting a settlement of late Iron Age or Roman times. Some Roman coins of the third century AD were also found.

The third main prehistoric feature is the Cross Dyke which runs across the top of the Common to the east from a point above the 'Staircase', one of the tracks which ascend from Rising Sun Lane. It is easily traced to its end, well down in Dry Bottom. This, too, is of uncertain date, but may also be of the Iron Age. It has all the appearance of a boundary marker and for very many years formed the boundary between the part of the Common belonging to Bishop's Cleeve and that belonging to Southam. In two places boundary stones can be found in it. They are marked with the reversed 'S' which is found on a similar stone lower down, above the end of Rising Sun Lane and which also marked the boundary of Southam. A solitary surviving stone can be found continuing the boundary across the Common to the south. They were all noted by the ordnance surveyor who recorded the parish boundaries in 1882.

Life of the Common

Having considered the topography and history of the Common we must now consider its living inhabitants, for it has a life if its own as an important habitat of a variety of living things.

Flora

As we have seen the Common is an area of unimproved limestone grassland and as such it retains a species-rich flora differing from that over the wall in Postlip Warren, which was partly ploughed up in the war, and regularly receives fertiliser. The difference is clear in autumn and early spring when the Warren is greener than the Common. On looking over the wall you see what looks almost like a monoculture of rye grass compared with the numerous species on the Common. A description of some grasses will be made in a later chapter.

The Common has at least two species counted as rarities nationally, the musk orchid and the limestone polypody fern. In 1987 the mountain everlasting, a small plant more often seen on northern mountains, was found on the Common for the first time since the 1930s.

Over 200 species of flowering plants have been reported on the Common and at least 175 species can be fairly easily found. The first to appear are the snowdrops in January near the boundary walls where they have no doubt escaped from gardens. These are followed by the celandines in February. In March the minute white stars of the whitlow grass, which is not a grass but a member of the Crucifer family, appear. Its tiny flowers are found in bare stony places close to the ground. About the same time coltsfoot and primroses appear. In stony

Woolly thistle.

places with thin soil are the short slender stems, narrow leaves, and yellow anthers of the spring sedge. In similar places is the short wood rush which has narrow leaves with long hairs at the base.

Later the bulbous and common field buttercups and cowslips appear. On the slopes above the main road may be found the lesser dandelion, a characteristic plant of dry pastures differing from the usual plant in its small size and finely cut leaves. As the season advances the numbers of flowers greatly increase. The yellow of bird's foot trefoil and rock rose, the purple of thyme and the speckled white of eyebright are characteristic. At least eight species of orchids can be found on the Common, beginning with the early purple in April. In a good year there may be large areas of common spotted orchids but their flowering is very unpredictable. The purple spikes of the pyramidal orchid are usually found easily but the small greenish musk and frog orchids are present in only a few areas of the Common. The bee orchid, whose flower markings and shape closely mimic a bumble bee, is highly distinctive. The fragrant orchid is another with purple flowers. The twayblade is green in colour and not easy to see, but distinguished by its two large leaves.

By July the flowering season is near its peak. You seem to wade through massive tufts of the tor grass with the tall upright brome waving in the breeze on the summit. Near the ground where the grass is shorter there are the clumps of 'pepper and salt', or squinancy-wort and on the flat dry plateau area particularly, the scattered plants of the white-flowered dropwort, superficially like its relative of wet meadows, the meadowsweet. At the edges of the quarries are the rough hairy plants of the viper's bugloss with their red and purple flowers. In similar stony areas the stiff pale yellow, dry petals of the carline thistle can be seen. Other thistles will be mentioned in a later chapter. In July, too, the plants which will go on flowering into September first appear. They include the harebell, the autumn gentian and clustered bellflower.

In the sandy areas the calcifuge plants are found. They include the little white heath bedstraw, the first of these to appear. Later are the yellow tormentil and, of course, the heather. This is often quite dwarf and where larger the young shoots are usually bitten back by the sheep. The common too has its share of poisonous plants, the deadly nightshade and henbane being sometimes found. The first of these is a large plant and has juicy but poisonous purple fruits. The henbane, a coarse, almost shrubby plant, has pale flowers with a beautiful network of purple veins in the petals.

As well as the flowering plants there are several ferns, particularly the uncommon fern, the limestone polypody, found on stony slopes, bracken near Huddlestone's Table and the male fern in Bentley Lane. The fungi include the St George's mushroom and fairy ring mushroom. Occasionally the delicious blewits is found. On some of the walls are fine growths of yellow lichen.

Birds

The common species of birds seen in fields and woods are not often seen on the Common. Instead there are the species which favour open country. The meadow pipit and skylark are the most likely to be seen. The pipit can be recognised by its flight. It flies up to a medium height and then tends to 'parachute' down to the earth. Both these birds nest on the ground and may not find the growth of the coarse grass to their liking.

The linnet is another bird of open country and heath. It can be seen in summer near the gorse bushes, the cock bird with his reddish breast singing his little song.

A special bird of gorse and heath is the stonechat, a few of which can still be seen on the gorse bushes. The male is unmistakable with his black head, white collar and chestnut underparts as he sits on the top of a gorse bush uttering his 'chat' call. Cleeve Common is the only place in east Gloucestershire where these birds still nest.

Of other birds the willow warbler and sometimes the 'reeling' note of the grasshopper warbler can be heard. An interesting bird once frequently seen nesting in the area is the wheatear, now seen only as a passage migrant in March and September. Mellersh in his *Treatise on the Birds of Gloucestershire* (1902), says these birds used to nest in the walls and quarries of the Common. He tells the interesting story that this bird, known locally as the 'Horsematcher', was well known to the quarrymen who greeted its appearance in the spring with a special toast to celebrate the passing of winter.

Other passage migrants seen on the Common are the ring ouzel on its way to wilder streams in the Pennines and Wales, and the dotterel making for the Scottish mountains.

Adder on Cleeve Common.

26

Musk orchid.

Of the more usual countryside birds the yellowhammer is fairly frequent and the kestrel can be seen hovering over the scarp on the look-out for insects and other prey, and buzzards are sometimes seen soaring.

The raven is an occasional winter visitor, identified by his loud croak as he flies over. Special reference will be made in a later chapter to the jackdaws and pigeons of the cliffs.

Other animals

Apart from birds and rabbits the animals of the Common are not often seen, being mostly nocturnal. Their presence can however be inferred from the traces they leave. As well as the obvious tracks made by humans the Common is criss-crossed by numerous animal tracks. Sheep following one another in single file make narrow tracks. In places these are so well used that the grass is worn away and the little cloven hoof-prints are visible on the bare earth.

Badger tracks show where these animals cross the Common or leave it by climbing over the stone walls. Here they can be traced by perhaps an obvious stain on the wall and by the presence of a few grey hairs on a strand of barbed wire. These animals, too, have the special habit of depositing their dung in pits or 'latrines' dug at special places. These pits mark the territorial boundaries of badger groups or mark their routes. Foxes do not seem to visit the Common frequently unless it is to catch rabbits which live in burrows in the sandier parts and make small runs close to them. Rabbit tracks are best distinguished in snow.

Deer of roe or fallow species may with luck be sometimes seen. The little muntjac is also known to inhabit the area. The grasslands are a resort of adders which lie up for the winter in holes and other sheltered spots and can sometimes be seen warming themselves in the spring sunshine. Though most unlikely to attack humans, dogs are known to have been bitten. If that happens to your dog veterinary advice should be obtained. Another snake occasionally seen is the bronze coloured slow worm.

Butterflies and other Insects

Like other parts of the Cotswolds, Cleeve Common is an important area for butterflies, especially blues. Several species of blue butterflies have a special relationship with ants on the ground. For example, the caterpillar of the chalkhill

blue produces a substance which attracts yellow meadow ants which cover it with soil, so perhaps concealing it from enemies. The large blue, once not uncommon in the vicinity of Cleeve Hill became extinct in Britain in the 1970s though attempts have been made to re-introduce it. Its caterpillars produce a special substance which attracts ants and make it indistinguishable from ant larvae. The ants carry the caterpillar into their nests and tend it through the winter, though it is parasitic on their larvae. The disappearance of this butterfly is related to changes in the grassland habitat, the large coarse grasses being less suitable for the particular species of ant necessary to the butterfly. Among other butterflies still to be seen are the small and common blues, the grayling, the marbled white, the meadow brown and the small skipper.

The tube webs of a spider are to be found close to the ground and there are still some of the hills produced by the yellow meadow ant though fewer than previously, probably again a consequence of the spread of coarse grasses. In the summer twilight glow-worm lights may be seen produced by the females which have climbed up to the top of grass stems.

The molluscs include a tiny rare snail, the large chrysalis snail (*Abidon secale*), which inhabits warm limestone grassland and is here at about the northern limit of its range.

This account has attempted to give an impression of the Common and its importance, but by no means are all aspects covered. Cleeve Hill and Common exemplify many of the problems of countryside conservation today. As a large area of the vanishing category of natural limestone grassland it is of great importance that it should be protected. Despite its legally protected status as an Site of Special Scientific Interest and the protection afforded by being within the Area of Outstanding Natural Beauty of the Cotswolds and with its own bye-laws, it is still subject to many threats of excessive or inappropriate use, and management is difficult. The growing demand for leisure activities by the greatly increased population of the Cheltenham area, now over 100,000, puts a strain on the resources of the Common. This is already seen in the erosion caused mainly by horse riders and golfers and illegal motorbike riding.

The Board of Conservators in conjunction with the Countryside Commission, and following the best modern practice, have recently (1992) appointed a firm of consultants to produce a management plan for the Common. Their report and recommendations are a landmark in the history of the Common and it is hoped will lead to a clearer understanding of its importance and ways of managing it. Funding has always been a problem, however, and new sources of finance may have to be found.

Part of the attractiveness of Cleeve Common is the sense of wildness and remoteness, especially on its eastern side. This would not survive much increased visiting by pedestrians, cyclists and riders. As in other places, increased numbers of visitors would destroy what they came to see.

The area has always aroused the strong emotional interest of the local people in various ways and its well-being is sought by the more concerned of them. Richard Mabey, in the book quoted at the beginning of this chapter, considers that the intricate feature of our landscape is the result of the weaving together of human and natural life over five millennia. Cleeve Common exemplifies this statement and provides a total experience of visual, landscape, historical and biological features which must be preserved for the benefit both of its natural inhabitants and for ourselves.

Chapter Three

The view from Cleeve Cloud

... he may range ...
Over the living landscape, from the edge
Of Malvern's flowing line, along the vale
Where distant Severn winds ...

Charles Parry, 1807, in T. D. Fosbroke,
A Picturesque and Topographical Account of Cheltenham (1826).

ALL ALONG the Cotswold scarp are many viewpoints looking westward over the Vale. Cleeve Cloud is one of the best and most easily accessible of them. The new indicator at the small car park on the Cheltenham–Winchcombe road, the B4632, gives some idea of the scene, but the really great views are only revealed by climbing higher up. From the larger car park in Wickfield quarry near the golf club it is a gentle climb to the top at 1043 ft. (317 m.). Here there is the toposcope or indicator put up by the Cheltenham Rotarians to commemorate their jubilee in 1971. This shows the main landmarks to be seen on a clear day.

The view from Cleeve impresses by its vast extent over the Severn Vale to the Malverns eighteen miles away, and by the good views of the Welsh hills to the south west and the Worcestershire and Shropshire hills to the north west. Perhaps it does not have the variety of scene with views over the tidal Severn which are obtained from viewpoints further south along the scarp, but these are limited in extent by the nearness of the Forest of Dean hills. The Cleeve view never fails to impress, especially when you come upon it suddenly, as when driving over the summit from Winchcombe, or on foot from the eastern side of the Common, especially towards sunset.

Perhaps the best time to see the view is on a clear, showery day in March or April when the south-west wind is bringing rain clouds up from the direction of Hay Bluff and the approach of a shower can be anticipated by half an hour. At the same time the beautiful details of the vale, its fields, woods, buildings and the waters of the lower Severn, may be illuminated by stray patches of sunlight. Alternating with the clouds, these patches of light show details not noticed at other times.

You may see the most impressive effects when a thunderstorm is coming up the vale. The dark clouds, the flashes of lightning, and the distant thunder make a dramatic scene. At any time it is the changing appearance with different lights and different weather effects that make the scene so interesting.

In the morning when the sun is in the east, the buildings of Cheltenham and the nearer villages show up best. The church towers or spires of Elmstone

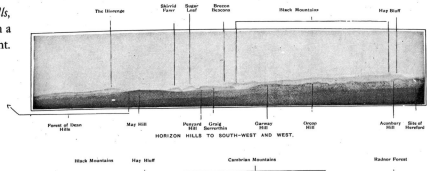

The Blorenge   Skirrid Fawr   Sugar Loaf   Brecon Beacons   Black Mountains   Hay Bluff

Forest of Dean Hills   May Hill   Penyard Hill   Graig Serrerthin   Garway Hill   Orcop Hill   Aconbury Hill   Site of Hereford

HORIZON HILLS TO SOUTH-WEST AND WEST.

Black Mountains   Hay Bluff   Cambrian Mountains   Radnor Forest

Aconbury Hill   Site of Hereford   Woolhope Hills   End of Malvern Hills

HORIZON HILLS WEST TO NORTH-WEST.

THE HORIZON HILLS AS VIEWED FROM CLEEVE CLOUD CLIFF, CLEEVE COMMON.

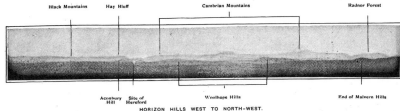

Herefordshire Beacon   The Malvern Hills   Worcestershire Beacon   North Hill

Site of Tewkesbury   Site of Great Malvern

HORIZON HILLS TO NORTH-WEST.

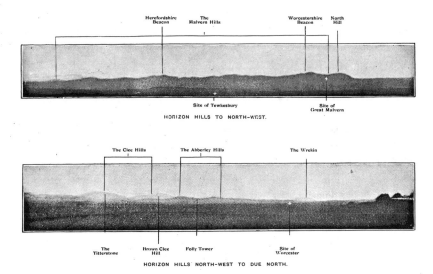

The Clee Hills   The Abberley Hills   The Wrekin

The Titterstone   Brown Clee Hill   Folly Tower   Site of Worcester

HORIZON HILLS NORTH-WEST TO DUE NORTH.

THE HORIZON HILLS AS VIEWED FROM CLEEVE CLOUD CLIFF, CLEEVE COMMON.

Hardwick, Deerhurst, Gloucester, Tewkesbury, Bishop's Cleeve, Upton and Bredon can all be identified. Later in the day with the sun higher, the Malverns are made to seem not so high as before and the buildings seen in the morning have slipped back into obscurity. In fact, the best time to see the outlines of the distant hills is often in the evening.

At other times all is softened by grey mists lying in the valley. These may make it easier to see the lesser, lower hills, Sarn Hill behind Tewkesbury,

Sandhurst and Wainlode hills near Gloucester, and others further away may be made to stand out from their background. Sometimes, but rarely, the whole vale is filled with a thick grey mist with clear air above, and only the tops of the hills are visible. We seem to be looking at a lagoon of mist with the islands of the Malvern chain floating on the far shore. A notable account of such a day as seen from Saintbury Hill in the north Cotswolds was given by Algernon Gissing in his book *The Footpath Way in Gloucestershire* of the 1920s.

Although the furthest Welsh hills are seen perhaps on only about sixty days a year, a feature is the speed of change that can happen. The limit of view may change from half a mile to fifty miles in half an hour.

Another feature of the view from Cleeve is the fact that, if no low clouds obscure the horizon, the point of sunset can be observed throughout the year. As seen from the area of the toposcope the sun sets on the longest day between the two northern-most hills of the Malvern chain, and its journey back towards its position on the shortest day over Robin's Wood Hill behind Gloucester, marks well the decline of the year.

The view of the town of Cheltenham and the nearest hills of the Cotswolds are better seen from the Iron Age camp half a mile further south along the Cloud from the indicator. From here the buildings of Cheltenham, with its towers and spires and three copper roofs, are seen. Behind and to the left of them the curve of Charlton Kings Common and Leckhampton Hill comes forward to the next

Telephoto lens view of Tewkesbury with Sarn Hill and the Malverns behind. Mist over the Severn.

steep part of the escarpment. Behind these the edge goes away with Painswick Beacon jutting forward into the vale. In front of it are two outliers, Churchdown Hill between Cheltenham and Gloucester, and Robin's Wood Hill between the city and the edge. The great tower of Gloucester Cathedral is to the right of Churchdown Hill and beyond and to the left of it can be seen the waters of the tidal Severn, especially if the tide is in. Bristol is hidden by higher ground bordering the Vale of Berkely, but the two towers of the Severn Bridge are visible, with in front of them the solid block of Oldbury nuclear power station.

Across the river on the western side, the border of the Forest of Dean is shown by the line of forested hills marked by the radio masts on Edge Hill. If the weather is clear the low mound of the Blorenge in Gwent can be seen. To the right again is the curve of May Hill, a hill of rocks of Malvern type, lying just outside the Forest and made unmistakable by the clump of pines on its summit. Next on the west, to the right, are a number of small hills in Gwent near Abergavenny. The first, with a sharp slope to the north-west, is Ysgyrid (Skirrid) Fawr. The next, with a conical shape, is the Sugar Loaf, named after the form in which sugar was formerly sold wholesale. In front and to the right of this is a long low hill, Graig Syfyrddin (Sererthin or The Graig). In front of this and best seen when a light mist separates it from the further, higher, hills is the low Penyard Hill, which has a steep slope to its northern side. The Graig lies in front of the two Brecon Beacons, the highest and furthest hills seen in this section. They are sixty-five miles away (105 km.) and only seen in the clearest weather. To the right again lies the long ridge of the Black Mountains ending in the steep slope of Hay Bluff above the town of Hay on Wye in Powys, forty-five miles away. To the right of Hay Bluff is the Wye valley and then there is a low ridge, Marcle Hill, on which is the very tall television mast, nineteen miles (30 km.) away, which rises above the ridge behind. Behind the mast and to the right again and much further away the Cambrian Mountains lie, ending in a rounded hill with a steep slope to the north, Radnor Forest. This lies behind the southern-most of the Malvern peaks, Chase End Hill.

The chain of the Malverns is the dominant feature of the view from Cleeve, as from many other viewpoints of the Cotswolds, and is more often seen than most of the hills so far described. Eighteen miles away this ridge of very ancient Pre-Cambrian rocks forms the boundary between the Severn Vale and the hills of Herefordshire. From Chase End Hill to North Hill it is eight miles long. The double-peaked hill near the centre is the Herefordshire Beacon and British Camp. The flattened hill top of the Iron Age camp is easily seen. The highest point of the chain, the Worcestershire Beacon, is next to North Hill. The houses of Great Malvern are seen clinging to the hillside and spread out along the road to the Wyche Cutting at the top where the road to Ledbury crosses. Midway in the vale between us and Malvern is the massive bulk of Tewkesbury Abbey, and to its right may be seen the spire of Upton on Severn church.

To the north of the Malverns there is a confused mass of low hills through which the River Teme runs. Far away beyond them rise two hills, the Clee Hills in Shropshire, forty-five miles (72 km.) away. They are volcanic intrusions into the plain and their basalt has provided hard roadstone for the area for many

Sunset, 22 June.

years. The one to the left is Titterstone Clee and has an air traffic radar and earth satellite installation on its summit, visible with a field glass in clear weather. In front of these and just to the right in our view, are the two Abberley Hills with the tall Folly Tower in the grounds of Abberley Hall between them. To the right of them again is the low mound of the Wrekin in Shropshire, fifty-five miles away. In front of it can be seen, with a field glass and in the right weather conditions, the vapour from the cooling towers of Buildwas power station on the Severn in the neighbourhood of Ironbridge.

To the left of this and much nearer is the mass of Bredon Hill, a Cotswold outlier, with the short tower on its westward end and a radio mast on its eastern. To the right of this the view extends away up the vale of Avon to the hills of Charnwood Forest in Leicestershire, before to the right again we come to Broadway Hill with its turreted tower on the Cotswold edge.

So much for the distant view. What of the nearer? Here there has certainly been deterioration over the last few years due to the growth of development in Cheltenham and Bishop's Cleeve. The light-coloured roofs of the buildings of the Swindon village industrial estate and at Bishop's Cleeve show the failure of the planning process when building is allowed without regard to the appearance from the hill. The buildings of Cheltenham, with one or two exceptions, form a pleasant whole as seen from the hills with their variety of roofs and spires and towers interspersed with trees. On the other hand the new buildings of Bishop's

Sunset, 19 December. Cleeve and Woodmancote with their man-made roofing tiles and stone compos-
ition walls look cold and monotonous. It remains to be seen if they will weather
to a more pleasing colour or be obscured by planting trees.

Nevertheless, considering that about one and a quarter million people live in
the area seen from Cleeve Hill, their impact is remarkably small. The rural
aspect is preserved by the distance and tree cover.

Mention must also be made of the scene at night. Far away the lights of
Malvern show the opposite side of the vale. To the north a string of lights shows
the M5 motorway, continued southwards by the lights of moving vehicles.
Across the centre are the lights along the Tewkesbury–Toddington road. Above
them shines the red aircraft warning light on Bredon radio mast. In the centre
of the vale have recently appeared the bright lights of a golf driving range. The
innumerable yellow lights at the foot of the hills lead to Churchdown Hill, also
with a red light, but smaller. In the same direction the lights along the ski slope
on Robin's Wood Hill show up to the east of Gloucester whose floodlit cathedral
tower stands out dully above the brighter city lights.

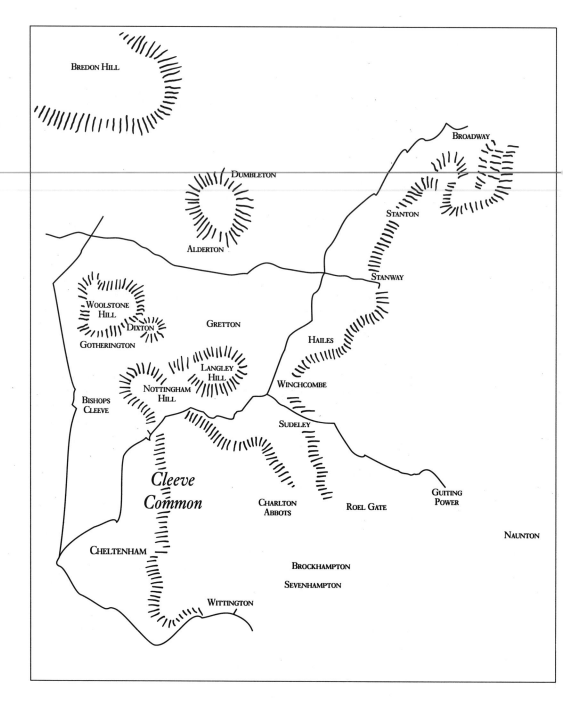

General relationship to one another of places mentioned in the text

Chapter Four

Walks over and round the Great Common

There is a breeze from the North West, the grass is clean and soft to the foot as ever, and the usual exhilaration is felt in breathing the keen, bracing air. As I come to the top strength and spirits seem to rise 100 per cent.

J. H. Garrett, *From a Cotswold Height* (1919).

CLEEVE HILL is one of the two points of the Cotswold scarp easily accessible from Cheltenham, the other being Leckhampton Hill. From the early years of the twentieth century it was reached from the town centre by electric tram which made it a popular place of residence and of recreation especially at bank holidays. The tram terminus was on the level stretch of road near the Malvern View Hotel. A short direct path called Tramway Alley, passing between the house gardens, connects the road here to the Common. Today public transport is provided by the bus service between Cheltenham and Winchcombe, but most people come by their own transport.

From Cheltenham the route goes along Prestbury Road with a view directly ahead of the three radio masts on the edge of Cleeve Common and a strip of woodland, Long Covert, on the slope to their right. To the left the quarry cliffs of Cleeve Cloud stand up on the highest part of the hill. The road then passes through the pleasant small village of Prestbury, now within the borough boundary, the buildings in the centre of which have changed little in seventy years. It then goes round a right-angled bend and soon reaches the area of the Cheltenham Green Belt. On the right is a farm house with a large holm oak. Both, though smaller then, were noted in the 1919 book.

Further on the road has park-like fields on the right which lead up to Queen's Wood on the slopes. On the left is the entrance to Southam Delabere house, now a hotel. This building has many Tudor features but was added to and altered in the nineteenth century by its most celebrated owner, Lord Ellenborough, for a short time Governor-General of India. Here an ancient trackway, Bentley Lane, on the right, leads up to the open Common by the side of Queen's Wood. This was named after the queen of Edward IV who was Lady of the Manor of Southam.

A little further on after the turnings to Southam and Woodmancote, the road starts to climb steeply with increasingly fine views of the vale until it reaches the Rising Sun Hotel, once a wayside inn, recently enlarged and modernised. Here a lane, Gambles Lane, comes up from the vale and leads on to the Common, though it does not form a good place for motorists' access as there is no parking place.

Further on after passing the youth hostel and two hotels, the road reaches an open area, Stockwell Common, where a small parking place and viewing indicator have been made. Here, where there is also an entrance to Cleeve Lodge Stables, is the only place where Cleeve Common actually touches the main road.

Further on the highest point of the road at 786 ft.(240 m.) is reached. Here an ancient track coming along the top of Nottingham Hill on the left, crosses and goes onto the Common. The driveable part of this leads to Cleeve Hill golf course clubhouse, and to a car park in an old quarry just within the Common.

The main road then descends into the valley of the Isbourne River in which lies Winchcombe. The view ahead is particularly pleasant with Langley Hill to the left, Winchcombe with its tower ahead and the wooded hills behind it bounding the valley towards Sudeley Castle on the right. The road leads down through the old grey stone houses of Winchcombe to the abbey terrace where a raised footwalk runs along the wall bounding the site of the abbey, of which no trace remains.

In the opposite direction, approaching Cleeve Hill from the north as many do, coming from Stratford and Broadway, the ascent from Winchcombe to the Nottingham Hill pass is not as steep as on the other side. Just over the top the view of the vale bursts suddenly upon one. Churchdown Hill near Gloucester is prominent ahead and to the right the flat vale extends to the Forest of Dean Hills and the Malverns. The scene is particularly fine towards sunset and at night there are vast numbers of glowing lights.

Probably not many of those who drive along this Cheltenham to Winchcombe and Broadway road over Cleeve Hill realise there is one and a half square miles of open country close by. The road passes along its edge for only a few hundred yards, but once you have started to walk over it, especially after climbing to the top, you realise what a marvellous and almost unlimited area for walking the Common is. It is still true, as in the quotation, that once up the short dry turf on the paths, the wide views and the breezes seem to create a new energy and you can walk for hours or miles.

These features ensured that the route of the long-distance footpath, the Cotswold Way, should pass over Cleeve Common. The way, as originally defined, it may be changed in the future, comes from the south, enters the Common between the radio masts and the Iron Age camp, passes along the edge of Cleeve Cloud cliff and descends to the youth hostel. It continues by exploring the valleys of the Common and leaves by the track which goes to Belas Knap Stone age barrow to the east.

Apart from the Cotswold Way walks long and short can be taken to all parts of the Common. For those who are interested in the natural world they can provide many attractions. In spring you may wander through the gorse or the tufts of long grass and suddenly come upon the spike of an early purple orchid. Nearer the ground are the yellow flowers of the spring sedge and the paler ones of the woodrush. A queen bumble bee may be flying close to the ground, in and out of the tussocks, probably seeking out a suitable place to make this year's nest and brood chamber. The meadow pipits fly up in dipping flight and then parachute down. Skylarks sing high above, the willow warblers sing their songs of descending notes from the bushes and the distant harsh call of a cock pheasant may be heard coming from the woods.

The five walks described here are a sample, visiting some of the most interesting parts of the Common. All, except number four, start from the Wickfield Quarry car park near the golf clubhouse (grid ref. so 989272). This is the only car park actually on the Common and is reached by taking the lane marked 'Municipal Golf Course' at the top of the hill and going over the cattle grid.

WALKS ON THE COMMON NO. I
Along by the Undercliff and back by the Camp.
About 3 miles (4.8 km.)

We will begin our exploration with a walk which will give at least one example of each of the main features the area is so rich in, archaeology, history, botany, geology, landscape, distant views.

Starting from the car park in Wickfield Quarry reached as described above, and from which stone was taken up to the Second World War, we walk down in front of the golf house, past the eighteenth green and practice ground of the Cleeve Hill Golf Course. Here the slope is crossed by shallow ditches and a long low mound which may be field boundaries made by the Iron Age peoples.

The track passes along the top of Jackdaw and Milestone quarries with a view over Bishop's Cleeve and Tewkesbury to the Malverns. It then descends past the third quarry which was already disused in the early nineteenth century, when the house and stables were built. The track we follow is the line of the first turnpike road from Cheltenham to Winchcombe made in 1792 which replaced

the ancient track over the hill. It was itself replaced by the modern road in 1823 and the houses were built between the two roads. The last house on this level, an older one, was extended to make the premises for the Cheltenham Golf Club and is now the youth hostel.

From above Rising Sun Hotel looking over Woodmancote and Bishop's Cleeve.

A little further on a level area backs the house made for the second club, the Cheltenham Artisans, now two private houses. In a corner of the Common near here are the high railings surrounding the pound put up soon after the Board of Conservators started to manage the Common in the 1890s and used for the containment of animals found on the Common without legal right.

From near here three clumps of trees can be seen, one of beeches, the Coronation or King's Clump, one of sycamores and chestnuts, and the lowest one of limes, the Winterbotham clump. These have been planted in the valley which runs up from the lane which reaches the Common at this point. The beeches were planted to commemorate the coronation of King Edward VII and just below is the site of the Romano-British settlement mentioned in chapter two.

The lane, Rising Sun Lane, is the continuation of Gambles Lane. It is one of the ancient lanes which come up to the Common from the vale and were used by graziers who held rights on the Common to bring up their cattle, and by quarrymen to bring stone down. The lane here passes between the Rising Sun Hotel and the turreted Little Castle. On the Common at its top is the memorial

Sheep's Fescue

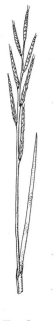

Tor Grass

horse trough. This now seems to commemorate not only the chairman of the Board of Conservators whose name it bears, but also those nameless men who worked in the quarries on the hill, and their horses for whom it was provided.

We take an upward climbing rough road here and soon pass on the right a stone walled field into which the quarry horses were turned after work. To the left lies the great scarp of Cleeve Cloud, rising about 100 feet above the track and to the right ahead is the dark mass of Thrift Wood.

As we climb the track we can look at the plants around us. No doubt most visitors to the Common give little thought to the plants on it. It is mostly just 'grass' to them and in winter it has a sere and rather dreary aspect. However if we look more closely at it as we climb this track, especially in spring and summer, we will find within the space of a square yard or so half-a-dozen different species of grass, not all in flower at the same time. The short grasses, which usually flower first, include sheep's fescue, sweet vernal grass and later, crested dog's tail. There are also the beautiful quaking grass and the tall upright brome. Coarser tufted grasses are cock's foot and tor grasses. The yellowish grasses characteristic of the Cotswolds in the summer are the tor grass and the yellow oat and hairy oat. These coarse grasses are avoided by the sheep except when young and can only be kept down by mowing as on the golf fairways or by cattle grazing.

With the decline of grazing and the reduction in the number of rabbits in the last forty years these coarse grasses have spread over the Common, dominating the scene in large areas.

The drawings in the margin show the characteristic features of four common grasses (not to scale).

The cliffs of Cleeve Cloud are old quarry workings and below them fallen stones litter the ground. Especially in winter the wildness of the scene with the high cliff and the tumbled masses of oolitic rock is unusual in south midland England and reminiscent of a Pennine moor. The highest part of the cliff here is Castle Rock, a favourite place for rock climbers to learn their craft and the only place where the rock is firm enough to give good holds. So important is it as one of the few good exposed rock faces for climbing in this part of the country that a little book has been prepared describing the routes up and across it in detail. Near here too is a small cave, or rather crack in the rocks. In January 1957 this was the centre of national attention as a caver got stuck there and was only rescued after fourteen hours' effort. The place is now changed by falls from above and is not recognisable.

On the right of the track is Thrift Wood which is one of the ancient semi-natural woods of the Cotswold scarp. At the next corner we can look down on the small settlement of Nutterswood. This isolated enclosure from the Common was first recorded in 1564, and until the mid-nineteenth century consisted of one house only. Later others were built, and in the early years of the twentieth century one was advertising holiday accommodation. What an experience for holidaymakers it must have been, coming from Cheltenham in the tram and then walking or being taken by horse and cart along the rough track to this remote spot!

Some of the old houses have been replaced by modern ones and considerably enlarged. The original house was no doubt built to take advantage of the spring which comes out here and still supplies the houses. Until recently these houses were mainly occupied by people who worked in the quarries or had other reasons for living on the Common but now, like in so many other places, these people have died out or moved away.

From here we can take the track between the top house and the undercliff and follow it in the direction it leads towards the ascent of the scarp about half a mile further on. In doing so we pass the point at which a bridleway, called Bentley Lane, comes up along the side of Queen's Wood from the main road at Southam. Here, on a patch of almost level ground at the edge of invading bracken, there is a massive block of stone known as Huddlestone's Table. This is distinguished from the other blocks of naturally fallen limestone around by being squared and having on its upper surface an inscription, now hardly detectable.

The stone is named after the Huddlestone family. The first Sir John was Constable of Sudeley Castle, Winchcombe, in the fifteenth century, and it is likely that one of his sons, also Sir John, built the great house of Southam Delabere just below here. He is said to have replaced an earlier, damaged, stone with the one that exists today.

This spot with its views of the vale below and the cliff above, just below the ancient camp, is an interesting one and it is not surprising that a legend is associated with it.

This legend relates that in 798 King Kenulf of Mercia started to build the abbey at Winchcombe, then a place of considerable importance. In November 811 the Archbishop of Canterbury, in the presence of King Kenulf, two other kings and many bishops and nobles, dedicated the abbey. Also present was Eadbert the former king of Kent who had been captured by Kenulf some fifteen years before and held prisoner. To celebrate the occasion he was given his freedom. The story relates that after the ceremonies Kenulf took his guests on a hunting expedition in the woods of the vale and at the end of it said farewell to them at this spot. Perhaps this is not so unlikely as it seems as the bridleway we have already noted is a very ancient road which comes up from the vale at this point, climbs to the top of the hill and connects with other roads going towards the east. The earliest account of the story I have been able to find is in an obscure little book of about the middle of the nineteenth century called *Antiquated Spots round Cheltenham* by one W. T. Newenham. He relates that he enquired of an old inhabitant whose ancestors had lived in the area for three centuries or more, who told him that the original stone commemorated a feast three kings of different parts of England had held there. Following this up Newenham studied the history of the area and developed the story about Winchcombe Abbey, but makes the occasion the foundation rather than the final consecration.

The story was seized upon by Victorian romantic writers, especially Mrs Dent of Sudeley, who records it in her *Annals of Winchcombe and Sudeley* of 1877, and illustrates it with an engraving of the scene. The earliest description of the stone so far found is in the *Gentleman's Magazine* for 1779. That journal often contains oddments of historical information and it has a drawing of

Upright Brome

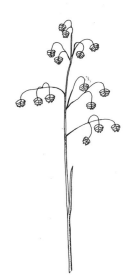

Quaking Grass

undecipherable marks on the stone's upper surface. There is, however, no mention of the legend. Later it was said to have had the words 'Huddlestone's Table' on it, but it is now difficult to make out anything. Whatever the truth of the legend, and it seems unlikely that a purely oral tradition can have survived a thousand years, it is a pleasant tale. The spot is certainly an interesting one, whether it was the meeting place of royalty in Anglo-Saxon times or just a picnic spot for the people of Southam Delabere in the sixteenth century.

This is a good place to pause and look around. Not only is there a fine view towards Cheltenham but the view of the cliffs behind is impressive especially late in the day when they are glowing in the light of the setting sun, the dark patches of ivy contrasting with the pale yellow rock. These rocks are the home of numerous jackdaws which nest on the ledges in the spring and fly out on anyone's approach. They seem more attractive birds than most members of the crow tribe, their cry of 'jack, jack' being pleasanter because more human and no doubt one reason why in the past they were occasionally kept as pets.

Near this spot are usually some of the thistles characteristic of the limestone. The most impressive Cotswold flower is surely the great woolly thistle with its large purple flowerheads on their globular bases, white with a close web of woolly hairs, and measuring two to three inches across when well developed. Another is the musk thistle, with its drooping head backed by large purple bracts and with a faint scent. A third variety in many places on the Common where the grass is short, is the dwarf or stemless thistle much disliked by picnickers and dogs as its rosette of spiny leaves, closely pressed against the ground, is not easily seen. Only if the single stemless flower head is present is it likely to be noticed.

From the level ground near Huddlestone's Table we climb up the steep yellow track to the plateau. When the top of the path is gained we are in a different country. The air is bracing, the view wider and this continues all the way along the edge. Near the top of this track two small beeches are growing. Their stunted and irregular growth in this exposed position shows the strength of the prevailing south-west wind. They are the two surviving trees of the Three Sisters mentioned in the 1919 book. Comparing them with the photograph in that book they hardly seem to have grown at all in seventy years. Perhaps their energies have been entirely spent in surviving in this place. A sentimental story has been made up suggesting that they mark the burial place of three sisters who, crossed in love, took up good works. In sight is another clump of beeches even smaller though further from the cliff edge. They are surrounded by a dilapidated iron fence which protected them in earlier years. Not far away, on the highest point of this part of the Common, is a single beech and from that place there is a good view of the surrounding country, from the towers of Bredon and Broadway in the north to the inner hills of the Cotswolds to the east and south.

Returning to the edge we come now to an area bounded by the cliff and the double ditches of the Iron Age camp. Once larger, its area has been reduced by quarrying and it has been altered by an entrance through the ditches to a golf green made when the course was constructed in the 1890s.

This camp is an important member of the string of Iron Age fortresses along the Cotswold edge which extend from Little Solsbury Camp, Batheaston, above the Avon, to the northern-most outlier on Meon Hill in Warwickshire. They were built by Iron Age peoples in the last millennium BC, about 1,500 to 2,000 years after the Neolithic people had made Belas Knap and the other long barrows. That some at least of these camps were indeed used as forts was clearly shown when excavations revealed evidence of a battle with the remains of many slain warriors at the camp on Bredon Hill.

Cleeve Hill camp is at a place where the cliff turns sharply which not only allows a piece of land to be isolated by the dykes but also gives a great view of Cheltenham with its towers and spires, and of the valley of the Chelt running into the hills, backed by the bare slopes of Charlton Kings Common on Leckhampton Hill. This view is not obtained from the area just outside the camp to the north.

Walking along the edge to the north we now look down on the tops of the trees in Thrift wood far below and out over the vale where Prestbury Park racecourse is prominent and, if the weather is reasonably clear, the Malverns and the Welsh hills. Growing from the rock just below here are several white-beam trees, a characteristic position for them.

We soon come to an area of shallow quarry excavations, called the Punchbowl Quarries, and may take the steep sunken track down towards the Rising Sun hotel and the houses of Cleeve Hill, or we may continue along the top across the Cross Dyke and directly towards the highest point being careful to avoid the golfers. This dyke is another ancient earthwork, a linear feature which runs eastwards from the scarp suggesting it marks a boundary. Though difficult to date, it is also attributed to the Iron Age and, as we have seen in chapter two, was later used to mark the parish boundary between Southam and Bishop's Cleeve. The northern part of the Common then lay in Bishop's Cleeve.

Soon after this the highest point of this part of the Common is reached at the Ordnance Survey's pillar and the toposcope or view indicator. The height of this point is 317 metres or 1,040 ft. above the sea. Contrary to popular belief this is not the highest point in the Cotswolds which is about one mile or two kilometres to the south on the part of the Common called West Down. This has a height of 330 metres or 1083 ft.

From the indicator we can descend following the Cotswold Way markers towards the youth hostel. This brings us near Cleeve Hill's third major earthwork, The Ring, an area enclosed by a circular bank and ditch but of uncertain date and purpose. The interior has been altered by being made into the eighteenth green of the first golf course laid out here. Just north of this is another small earthwork mound or tumulus, almost lost in the invading gorse.

Just below the gorse is a grassy track which runs almost level to two old quarries, Rolling Bank and Freestone, separating them from the grass grown spoil heaps which are characteristic of this part of the hill. The first and smaller of the two, Rolling Bank, though now largely grass-grown, is a mecca for geologists as it contains a hard limestone rock, the Phillipsiana beds, found nowhere else. This quarry also used to have the best fossils on the Common. From here it is an easy downhill walk to the golf clubhouse and car park in Wickfield quarry.

WALKS ON THE COMMON NO. 2

Postlip, the Washpool and up to the View
About 4 miles (6.5 km.)

From the golf club house a track leads north-eastwards along the edge of the Common. This is part of the old Winchcombe road built in 1792 to improve the communication between Cheltenham and that town. Until then it had been little better than a packhorse track over the high ground of the Common. The details of its route are described in chapter two.

As we go along it we can see some of the characteristics of an early turnpike road, with shallow pits from which stone was taken for repairs close alongside in places. We go down the gentle slope with views of Cockbury cottages and their rookery in tall tress across the stud farm paddocks to the left, with Langley Hill beyond. Down in the valley the tower of Winchcombe church shows up prettily over the older part of the town, which if it spreads further will spoil the view.

We pass alongside the fairway to the first green to reach a gate near some sheep pens. This is the scene of great activity for a few days in October when the sheep are being sorted into their owner's flocks to be taken off the Common.

At a gate here the road leaves the Common, passing between fields on the left, and the piece of arable called Oat Piece encroaching into the Common on the right. Here scrub thorn and elder and other bushes have grown up and the roadstone pits are a colourful sight in July, with many varieties of wild flowers including the purple, pyramidal and bee orchids in good years. Here too vetch, knapweed and scabious flowers abound and the shiny bracts of the latter persist into November. The shrubs of hawthorn and sloe give cover to many birds especially willow warblers and yellowhammers and in autumn the numerous berries provide a food supply for the fieldfares and redwings from Scandinavia. On the open arable of the fields the red-legged or french partridge may be seen in winter.

At the end of this part of the track we come to another gate out on to the Common above Postlip Wood (grid ref. so 999272). This spot is particularly attractive. You look down the slope along the rough yellow road going south-wards to where the slopes of the Common and Postlip Warren close the view. To the left the road is bounded by woodland which hides Postlip Hall and is mostly beech but with some larch trees further on. Beyond fields stretch to the dark mass of Corndean Woods and to the left is the Sudeley Valley with its hill and farms. The castle of Sudeley, its honey-coloured stone just visible over the nearer trees, completes the view.

On the right the steep slope of the Common traversed by a level green path above the valley, falls to the yellow track. It seems to be the combination of unspoilt wildness with the rough man-made track which gives this place its special beauty and interest. Below is the original road from Cheltenham to Winchcombe which came over the Common and was used up to the end of the eighteenth century. Part of the interest of this place lies in this fact. You can imagine it being used by travellers over the centuries and the scenery here has not changed much since their time. Usually there are no humans in sight, at

most a rider or two or an occasional rambler. In autumn the russet leaves of the beeches on the trees and on the ground below them further beautify the scene. The trees of the nearest wood are frequently festooned with the old man's beard, or wild clematis, and in autumn with the low sun in the south-east their feathery fruits are lit from behind and give a silvery iridescence to the scene.

From the gate the track to the left goes off the Common through another gate and further on joins the main road to Winchcombe. We will take the track to the right and go down to the wall along the edge of Postlip Wood.

We leave the Common through another gate at a corner of the wall and walk more closely along the boundary wall of the grounds of Postlip Hall. This sheltered spot in the folds of the hills was recorded in Domesday and has been inhabited for at least 1,000 years. In the grounds, and seen over the wall, is a small private chapel, dating from the twelfth century when it was put up for the use of the people of Postlip. After falling into decay and being used as a farm building it was rediscovered in the 1880s, restored and rededicated to St James, and is used occasionally for Roman Catholic services. It still shows Norman features, especially in some of the windows and in the fish-scale ornamentation over the door.

The path leads round the high wall of the grounds of Postlip Hall, goes through several gates and eventually leads to Winchcombe along the river Isbourne. The hall is Tudor with six imposing gables. On the death of the last owner in the 1960s the hall was divided up into multiple apartments run as a co-operative carrying on several crafts.

In front and below the hall is a large tithe barn. On the end of the west gable of this is the figure of a man said to be Sir William de Postlip, who built the chapel. Like many other such figures it has a legend or tall story attached to it

The sheep wash in use before 1919.

which amused people in less sophisticated times than our own. This one says that Sir William descends to the stream to drink on the stroke of midnight!

We turn back past the modern stables, take a stile by an iron gate to the left, pass through another field and climb up above the stream to reach a stile onto the Common above a large spring. Turning left along a level path we soon reach the bottom of the deep combe down which the main stream comes. Here it is dammed to form a small pool and just below is the stone sheep wash. Made in 1897 a few years after the Board of Conservators of Cleeve Common was established it was used, like many others in the district, for washing sheep before shearing. Wool from washed sheep could be sold at a small premium which made the process worth while.

Water from the pool was allowed to run into the stone basin through a system of pipes and valves, sheep were thrown in one by one, their heads pushed below the surface for a second or two and then they scrambled out up the sloping walk way. The need for this procedure ceased after about 1950 when mechanical cleaning of the fleeces became available. The dam arrangement has been altered in recent years and the basin cannot now be filled.

The pool is the only sizeable piece of water on the Common and is sought by the sheep in hot weather. It was once deep enough to swim in but has silted up. From here several paths lead. We can climb steeply up to the old quarry overlooking the pool and close to the boundary wall with Postlip Warren.

This is separate from the Common and privately owned. It is interesting, however, to look over the wall and see the differences from the Common. The warren was ploughed up and sown with grass sometime in the last fifty years. As a consequence the sward is practically a monoculture of rye grass, unlike the varied grasses and other plants on the Common side of the wall. It is grazed by sheep for most of the year and treated with fertiliser. These facts account for its greener appearance than the Common but the great variety of plants was lost.

If we continue to walk up the bottom of the valley we notice the stony wildness of the combe. A strong spring comes out about 100 yards above the pool and in wet weather there are others on the valley side. This is the source of the River Isbourne which flows northwards to join the Avon near Evesham.

These springs show the line where the impervious clay below causes the water which has percolated through the porous limestone above to issue out. This spring line is a feature of Cotswold valleys and has determined the position of many villages.

Rushes and other water plants grow along the stream but above the springs these plants cease and we are back with the dry ground flora of most of the Common. The steep slopes are made wilder by the old quarry workings above, with tips of the grey shaley stone waste.

Towards the top, Watery Bottom as this combe is called, or Washpool Valley by those who walk the Cotswold Way, divides into two. We take the right hand fork and passing a few thorn trees gain the old track, called the White Way, which runs north to south across the whole length of the Common. We follow it to the right until it crosses the other valley, Dry Bottom, near the tenth golf green and eleventh tee and begins to climb.

A few yards up a path leads to the left to reach the Cross Dyke. This simple linear earthwork runs east and west and forms a convenient way to the west but as it crosses a golf fairway golfers must be looked out for. You suddenly come to the crest of the scarp and look out over the vast extent of the vale. This is quite an exhilarating change after walking over the Common with its nearer views. Even if the weather is moderately misty the contrast is marked with Cheltenham and Bishop's Cleeve below you. On clearer days all the details of the Vale to Malvern eighteen miles away and beyond can be seen.

Walking to the right from the end of the Cross Dyke the high point of this part of the Common is reached at the toposcope and Ordnance Survey pillar where most people come to see the view. From there the walk is completed along the side of the seventeenth fairway to the stony track and back to the clubhouse and Wickfield quarry car park.

Walks on the Common no. 3
*Along the whole length of the Common by
the White Way—West Down—Wontley Farm
About 7 miles (11 km.)*

The ancient track southwards from the golf course or Wickfield entrance onto the Common passes right through the whole length of the Common. This is the White Way and is the continuation of a very ancient road which, as described in chapter two, comes up from the vale at Gotherington and on its way crosses the Iron Age camp on Nottingham Hill. After crossing the Common it goes on to the villages of Sevenhampton and Brockhampton and joins with other old roads to the south and east.

From the Wickfield entrance to the Common the white track rises gently to the side of the old Freestone Quarry at the top where the elevation is 972 ft.(295 m.) (grid ref. SO 988267). Over the crest the way used at present descends through the gorse bushes towards the tenth golf green at the top of Dry Bottom but a much older track runs beside it a little lower down the slope, deeply hollowed into the hillside and long since abandoned as a way. Such alternative tracks are common along the line of ancient roads. When one became impassable another was used.

From the top you get an impression of the great extent of the open Common stretching to the radio masts one mile away. Immediately in front and not far away is the opposite side of Dry Bottom, the valley which has no water in it on the Common. The slope shows the scars of many old quarries and their tracks. It must once have been a busy place when the quarries were working. Now it is perhaps best seen after a heavy fall of snow when the outlines of the scars are smoothed and the whole has an air of unviolated whiteness and purity. One of the tracks opposite is dramatically cut by a quarry which must have been made after the road had fallen into disuse, probably when the quarries further on had ceased to be used.

The track along the bottom is another part of the old road across the Common to Winchcombe we noticed in the last walk, and goes along the wall of Postlip Hall grounds. As mentioned in chapter two this road is shown on John Ogilby's road book of 1675 as part of the road from Gloucester to Coventry. It came up from Prestbury and crossed the track we are on at the top of this valley. This is probably the place marked as Barnard's Cross on eighteenth-century maps of Gloucestershire.

Continuing past the green on our right the ground is covered with spreading gorse bushes like many other parts of the Common where the soil is sandy. They make a marvellous picture when in flower in May. On a calm warm day their heady peach-like scent fills the air.

In some places among the gorse may be seen the stonechat, the cock bird distinguished by his black head and rusty breast. He utters his cry, like two stones knocked together, from the top of a bush. Beyond here one is alone in the open spaciousness of the Common except for an occasional rider and distant golfer. This is the habitat of the skylark and the meadow pipit, the most frequently seen bird on the Common. Both are ground-nesting birds and sing in flight but the song of the lark is continuous and from a much greater height than the meadow pipit's which sings for a short time, then descends with a parachute-like flight.

The radio masts may seem an ugly intrusion but they form a useful landmark in this part of the Common where the ground is flat and featureless. This flat plateau has long been used for racehorse training. It was the scene of the first Cheltenham Races in 1819–30, 1835–42 and 1855. Great crowds were attracted here and their rowdy activities were denounced by the Cheltenham clergyman

of the time, the Rev. Francis Close. Later the racecourse was moved to the more accessible Prestbury Park.

The track up to Wontley Farm.

In winter when the gallops are in use, their line is marked with posts or red discs which add a sense of purpose to this part of the Common. Off our direct route but to the right, between the masts and the camp, is a shallow fold in the ground with the evocative name of Gipsy Hollow. In this secluded and sheltered spot gipsy caravans used to camp.

From near the masts may be seen, about a mile away to the left, a low, green, whaleback mound against the dark background of a wood on the horizon. This is Belas Knap, the Stone Age long barrow.

At the masts is another major entry point for walkers and riders at the end of the road from Cheltenham via Hewletts (grid ref. SO 994248).

Further on, near the wall on the right or west side, is the Ordnance Survey's pillar marking the highest point in the Cotswolds at 1071 ft. (330 metres). The boundary wall of the Common on the left, south east, now comes within less than a hundred yards of the wall on the south west and this narrow extension of the Common runs south-east for over a mile. This is West Down and is an interesting feature. It is probably best accounted for as waste ground beside the track, left open when the common field of Sevenhampton was enclosed. Commons elsewhere in the country have similar prolongations along roads crossing them. Another example on Cleeve, now much overgrown, is the one along the ancient way coming up from Bentley Lane, Southam.

We walk beneath the electricity transmission lines, and note a track leading off to the right. This leads westward and, with a slight deviation to the left along the road from the Hewletts, before turning right again, comes out on the top of the scarp overlooking Prestbury, with a view of the vale towards Cheltenham and Gloucester. This track is probably one of those used by the parliamentary army on its way from Stow on the Wold to relieve Gloucester when it was besieged by King Charles I. A graphic contemporary account exists of the events. It was considered unwise for the heavy wagons and guns to go down the 'very craggy, steep and dangerous hill' in the dark, so the army encamped above Prestbury for the night of 5 September 1643. Even so there was much difficulty and some wagons were overturned.

The night was one of rain and storm and it is said the army, which consisted mainly of recently joined London trained bands, got their first experience of the rigours of military life here encamped without shelter on the hilltop.

Continuing our walk along West Down we come to the Brockhampton gate. Here a rough road crosses on its way to Wontley Farm and Winchcombe. This road, coming from Brockhampton and Whittington villages, was called Racecourse Road when the races were held on the Common. Before it reaches the Common it passes the remains of old slate pits. This was one of the places, usually at the edge of the Greater Oolite geological formation, where stone suitable for Cotswold slates was once quarried.

The track to the end of West Down continues as a grassy way through an increasingly dense tangle of hawthorn, briar and other scrub bushes, demonstrating what happens when grazing ceases. It is a wild but attractive place, the haunt of small birds in summer and full of bright berries in autumn. Since this was written much of this area has been affected by fire and its future is uncertain.

Eventually we reach the gate marking the end of the Common and enter a track running between walls with arable fields on either side. This must have been a pleasant way in the early part of this century, with views over the walls before the scrub trees grew up. Someone seems to have planted whitebeam trees at regular intervals along it. Their white-backed leaves and red berries in autumn still provide an added interest.

To the left, in the valley, can be seen West Wood which in the early nineteenth century came up to the track which now turns left downhill. Here again evidence of its antiquity and frequent use is shown by the existence of a holloway which runs parallel, hidden in the wood on the right.

On reaching a metalled road we turn left soon passing a cottage orné and pass through the valley with woods on each side and an arable strip in the middle. The wood on the right is full of bluebells in spring. This cool damp valley is the place for the autumn meadow saffron whose mauve flowers can be found in the grass beside the road. At the top is West Wood House, formerly a farm, and we come out into the open of the Wontley valley.

The path goes up this pleasant green valley passing a great oak and soon the large empty buildings of the ruined Wontley Farm are seen ahead. This settlement was recorded in 1166; it had six tenants in 1182 and later became pasture. In the 1930s and '40s the land was worked from West Wood and the house occupied by farm workers. The pulley wheel, which survives on the wall, was part of the machinery for milling grain for cattle feed. In the mid-twentieth century its remote situation could no longer provide the amenities expected for our time and it was abandoned. The house was pulled down to prevent illegal occupation.

Four tracks cross here and it is the place where a decision about whether or not to visit the Stone Age long barrow of Belas Knap must be made. We will leave that to the next walk and continue up the shallowing valley straight ahead, walking along the edge of an arable field until we reach the gate and come onto the Common again. We are now in the upper part of the third of its valleys, Padcombe Bottom (grid ref. SP 001247).

From here we can walk north westward by a path through the gorse, reaching the old track near the radio masts, or, following the waymarked Cotswold Way, reach the top of Watery Bottom and follow it to Postlip with a nice view of Winchcombe in the distance. From there the return to the car park is the reverse of the direction we took in walk two.

WALKS ON THE COMMON NO. 4
From the masts across the Common to Belas Knap
and back by Corndean, Postlip and the Washpool
About 8 miles (12.75 km.)

From Cheltenham another way of driving to the Common is by taking Harp Hill, at the junction of Hales and Hewlett roads, and driving up past Hewletts reservoirs. The road then goes steeply up Agg's Hill. At the top it bears right with a field on the left and reaches a cross roads where it turns left. From here a straight road leads to the radio masts and the gate onto the Common (grid ref. SO 994248). Here a small car park has been provided. On the way there is a good view of Cheltenham race course far below, and the vale away to the Malverns. Near the masts an old road comes up from Noverton and Prestbury by a sunken way beside a beech wood.

At the masts' gate one seems to be looking out to sea so flat and featureless is the plateau with an open horizon in front. This is the area of the racehorse training gallops and the old racecourse. Old maps show a figure-of-eight race-course here and today this, together with a straight gallop, is used by the trainers. The right to use this area is limited to those who have taken out a special racehorse training licence with the Board of Conservators. The race horses are there almost every morning from September to April and the area is not suitable for ordinary riders at that time. When the gallops are in use a warden is present in the area.

The gallops, when in use, are marked by coloured markers or posts which form useful points of reference in the featureless area. Walking a little way from the gate brings more distant parts of the Common into view. We will go straight ahead from the gate and slightly to the right. This will lead us by the edge of a small depression, the Cockpit, a spot perhaps once used for the long since illegal sport of cockfighting. Following the grassy track we come to the main path of the Cotswold Way and turning to the right go down through the gorse bushes to the top of Padcombe Bottom, the valley which runs north-eastward along the edge of the Common. Here there is a gate in the wall of the Common leading to the track for Wontley Farm (grid ref. SP 001247).

Padcombe Bottom is the third of the valleys on the Common and the most remote. From this point it soon deepens and the side towards the Common becomes increasingly steep. The other side is covered by the wood of Breakheart Plantation and scrub. This makes the valley rather gloomy, especially as the path leading out of the Common through the woods is little used.

We take the track leaving the Common through the field gate and follow the Cotswold Way leading east, along the edge of the field towards Wontley Farm. These upland fields are usually planted with oil seed rape, brilliant yellow in early summer, or other arable crop, and give a good view of the surrounding country. Ahead and to the left we can see a low green mound at the edge of a wood—our immediate objective, the long barrow of Belas Knap.

The buildings of the deserted Wontley Farm appear ahead and have been described in walk three. We turn left up the hill with a view down the valley to West Wood. Soon we come to a plateau again where the road passes between stone walls and bushes over the high wold. A signpost shows the path to the right alongside a wall across a field to Belas Knap. The mysterious long green whaleback mound is now much nearer. Eventually we enter its enclosure over a stile.

Belas Knap—the name means Beacon Hill—is one of the most interesting spots on the Cotswold Way and one of the best examples of a neolithic long barrow on these hills. It was built by Stone Age people and excavation has shown signs of an early neolithic burial beneath the present mound. This was the earliest time the site was used, about 2,900 BC. The mound we see is of the middle neolithic, 900–2400 BC. It lies roughly north-south, is 175 ft. (53 metres) long and 18 feet (5.5 metres) high. It has a forecourt at its northern end with a 'false portal' made of large stones. The barrow was first excavated in 1865 and again in the 1920s. The 1919 *From a Cotswold Height* has a photograph of it in about 1914 showing the state it was left in by the early excavators but with a large amount of dry stone-walling remaining in the forecourt, unchanged since neolithic times. In 1927-8 the walling was restored, giving the tidied-up appearance now seen but the lower layers at least of these thin flat stones are still those put up by the Stone Age people some 4,000 years ago.

The burials were in four chambers in the sides and lower end of the mound. The remains of about thirty-eight bodies were found as well as those of six children in the material blocking the false entrance. Although it is easy to surmise that the forecourt was used for ritual purposes we can only guess at what went on. What is clear, however, is that the mound was highly significant to these early peoples as they must have put an enormous effort into making it. It has been estimated some 15,000 man-hours would have been spent on its construction. A similar long barrow at Hazelton has been completely dismantled and shown to have a complex structure with internal walls to ensure stability.

This place also had attractions for the later Bronze Age people for one of their round barrows was built a few yards away in the field to the south-west. Unfortunately, since this field was converted to arable the barrow has been practically destroyed by ploughing. Further evidence of early human activities is given by the scattered flints found in nearby fields. These are not derived from the local rocks and must have been brought in by the prehistoric inhabitants.

Whatever went on there in the distant past, the spot is now a pleasant one for a pause in the walk—at least when its peace is not shattered by low flying aircraft. We leave by the Cotswold Way which runs beside, then through, part of Humblebee How Wood. A pleasant evocative name, Humblebee, but place-name scholars say it means 'scarred hill'.

Down the path we soon reach the metalled road near a spot where there is space to park cars under some old and twisted ash trees. We turn left and left again at the corner going along a lane which leads beside the mostly coniferous Breakheart Plantation with good views of Winchcombe church tower in the valley to the right. Where the road forks we go right. Soon drives lead to the extensive buildings of the eighteenth-century Corndean Hall. Continuing along the road there are a variety of woodland plants colourfully lining it in summer. The most obvious is the rosebay willow herb whose purple clumps occur where small clearings allow it to thrive. In late summer its feathery fruits are carried away in any breeze, scattering its seeds far and wide.

At the end of the metalled road where it turns to a cottage deep in the woods, there is a gate and stile at the top of a bridleway down which we turn to the right (grid ref. SP 008263). This descends steeply with a grassy meadow to the right of it. In early summer I have seen this meadow quite white with the flowers of the ox-eye or moondaisy. At the bottom in a dell shaded by hazel and other trees, and with the ground covered by the dark green plants of the dog's mercury, is a small stream, the furthest waters of the Isbourne. It is crossed by a few rough stepping stones and the path climbs up to open fields. On the left is part of Postlip Warren the other side of which we have so often seen from the Common. A little further on a large set of modern farm buildings shows why old buildings are not very suitable for modern farming. The great multi-purpose shed can accommodate cattle in winter as well as hay and straw and farm machinery. To the right looking down the Isbourne valley the flags flying from Postlip paper mills are also signs of the wider modern world. The iron-free waters of the stream are ideal for paper making and this has been carried on here for at least two centuries, though the modern process is rather different from the old.

Just past here is the best view of Postlip Hall, its six sharp gables straight ahead. A late sixteenth- or early seventeenth-century building it is a typical Cotswold large house. The small building behind is St James's Chapel.

We turn left before the bridge and walk beside the great high wall of the hall grounds. This wall is built of stone blocks without cement for the most part. Between it and the hall is the great barn. Over a patch of damp ground through two gates and past the stables we take a stile on the left and head up the bank above the stream to reach a stile onto the Common just above a spring, as in walk two. We are now at the foot of Dry Bottom. We turn left to reach the Washpool. This time we will continue up the wild stony valley and take the larger left-hand fork ahead which will bring us through the gorse out on to the plateau.

An interesting alternative from the end of Dry Bottom is to take the steep sunken road leading up to the top of the old quarries, go to the White Way and then towards the masts. The radio masts make a prominent landmark to walk towards to reach the road end.

Another alternative when we have climbed up Watery Bottom a little way is to follow the Cotswold Way marker and turn sharp left up the slope to get a good view of the valley from the old quarry workings. From there the way leads towards the Wontley gate where we joined it first.

WALKS ON THE COMMON NO. 5
The northern part of the Common.
Postlip Gate—the High Path to Dry Bottom—up to the toposcope
About 2¼ miles (4 km.)

If we want a short walk there is an interesting one round the north and north-eastern parts of the Common. It can be started from the Cotswold Way sign on the White Way track a little above the Wickfield quarry car park at the golf club entrance, or by walking directly above the car park quarry to the grassy track. This is followed above the third golf fairway just below the gorse bushes to the irregular ground of shallow quarries and sand pits where there is a good view of the Vale of Evesham and Langley, Bredon and Alderton hills. The ground here is made up of the Harford Sands which have been mentioned as a characteristic feature of Cleeve Hill in chapter two. They were probably derived from a sandy shallow sea in Jurassic times and occur in a few places in the Cotswolds. As we have mentioned they have an important effect on the vegetation. Their porosity means that calcium salts from the limestone seeping into them are soon leached out enabling some plants to grow which are usually only found in acid, calcium-poor, soils. These plants include the little white heath bedstraw and heather. This last is particularly interesting and it can be seen in a dwarf form on this part of the Common near the fourth tee.

This area of sand pits may well have been the place from which it is reported sand was taken by strings of pack-donkeys to the Staffordshire potteries. That must have been quite a sight!

Near here there are two memorial seats which have a good view towards Winchcombe and Sudeley. Going to the furthest part of the hill there is a rough track going down towards Winchcombe in the distance. The field on the left here, called Oat Piece, was enclosed from the Common at some distant date, probably in the eighteenth century. It is usually in some arable crop.

Keeping Winchcombe straight in front the rough path goes where there are lines of many ruts in the grass tufts, perhaps showing that this was one of the alternative routes of the road over the Common between Cheltenham and Winchcombe. We soon come to the junction of ways at the Postlip gate described in walk two (grid ref. SO 999272).

From here there is a choice of ways. One is to return directly to the quarry car park by going through the gate on the left and along the old Winchcombe road. Another is to turn back, right, south-westwards, and take the level track above the valley. This gives nice views down to Postlip and Corndean. On the top of Postlip Warren opposite can be seen the memorials in the private burial ground of a former owner of the hall and members of the family. Below our path are several lunging circles in the grass which are the places used for training young horses. A little way along this level track a narrow old cart track to the right leads to a couple of small quarries called Side Slope quarry and along this south-facing slope in summer are a number of plants usually including several orchids and the autumn gentian. Opposite are the old Postlip quarries and their various tracks. The level path meets the one coming up along Dry Bottom which is the main line of the ancient road from Cheltenham to Winchcombe. On the further side of the valley are clumps of limestone polypody fern, their dark stems persisting in winter until the new season's growth appears in spring. This track meets the White Way at the embankment at the top of the valley and we then turn right and walk up to the top where the shallow quarry contains a shed. If we want to prolong the walk we can go left here alongside the golf fairway to the toposcope on the top of the hill and then back along the scarp edge to Freestone quarry and the White Way to the car park quarry.

Chapter Five

Walks not on the Common

Here I left the main road by the wide lane that runs between stone walls on the left along the top of Nottingham Hill. Over the ridge of the hill a breeze was moving, bringing up trooping clouds out of the South-West, that sailed under the blue sky high above both vale and hill ...

J. H. Garrett, *From a Cotswold Height.*

FROM THE Stockwell Common car park on the Winchcombe road, the B4632, the side of the hill opposite is separated by a valley closed at the top by the ridge which connects Nottingham Hill with Cleeve Hill. Along this ridge Wickfield Lane runs from the main road to the top of Nottingham Hill. The part of the hill overlooking Woodmancote is called Holder's Hill. On the slope of the hill to the west is Bushcombe Wood, and just round the corner of the hill is the village of Gotherington, lying at the edge of the vale. The whole area can be explored by two easy walks.

1. Round Nottingham Hill (2 miles, 4 km.)

Wickfield Lane is the turning to the left at the top of the main road where it becomes double track for a short distance (grid ref. SO 989275) The lane has a wide strip of roadside waste suitable for parking. This is part of the ancient way, dating at least from Anglo-Saxon times which, as we have seen in chapter two, comes up from Gotherington and passes southwards over the whole length of Cleeve Common.

Just before this lane starts to go steeply downhill to the left, an unmetalled track runs straight ahead through a gate, leaving the road to Wickfield farm on the right, and goes through some rough woodland to the place where the banks of Nottingham Hill camp cross it. The road, now Granna or Grinnell Lane, runs straight and nearly level between stone walls across the top of the hill with views ahead and to the right. The walls were probably made when the Common on the top of the hill was enclosed in 1808 but the track follows the old line.

Nottingham Hill camp, one of the largest Cotswold camps, 120 acres in extent, is formed by the double bank and ditches cutting off the promontory of the hill whose steep scarp slopes make the other borders. Assumed to be of Iron Age date, two bronze swords and other relics were found here in 1972. It is mentioned in the Anglo-Saxon charters as Cocca's Burgh, a name persisting in the area as Cockbury.

The roadside here in July is full of a great variety of limestone wild flowers, knapweed, hedge parsley, burnet saxifrage, cow parsley, scabious, catchfly, wild mignonette, vetches. Sometimes there are a few patches of sainfoin, the pinkish pea-like plant once widely cultivated in the Cotswolds for animal fodder.

At the end of the walls, about a mile from the main road, the track starts to descend and splits into three ways at a gate. To the right the old way becomes a holloway and reaches the Gotherington–Winchcombe road in about three-quarters of a mile (1.25 km). Straight ahead a path leads below the abandoned farm to Gotherington manor and village, and to the left, above the farm, a path leads round the hill.

Before we take this last choice we can pause at the gate and look over the vale as this is one of the best places to see the outlying hills and their details make a nice view. Straight ahead lies the north end of the Malvern chain and to its right are the two Abberley, and still further away the Clee, hills. Nearby is Oxenton-Woolstone Hill, rising above the villages of those names, This has a dark patch of wood on its right or eastern side where it is separated from the smaller, bare-topped Dixton Hill by a valley. This hill's curious shape once thought to be an old fortified place, is now considered to be due to geological causes. It is just above the sixteenth-century house of Dixton Manor which can be seen when leaves do not obscure it.

Behind Oxenton is the long mound of Bredon Hill with its stumpy tower at its higher, western (left-hand) end and the radio mast at its nearer, eastern end. To the left again Tewkesbury tower is visible. To the right of Dixton is the larger Alderton-Dumbleton Hill with dark woods on its upper slopes. To its right again may be picked out the spiky nineteenth-century Gothic pinnacles of Toddington Manor and the spire of the church. Beyond them the open vale goes away to Evesham and the Lench Hills. On some days you may see a moving plume of steam and smoke from the revived steam railway between Gretton and Winchcombe.

To the right the Cotswold edge runs by Hailes and Stanway to Broadway with its tall tower. Beyond this again, if the weather is at all clear, is the northern-most outlier of the Cotswolds, Meon Hill, not far from Stratford on Avon.

Through the gate we take the path curving to the left and going just above the ruins of Gotherington Farm where, at least until recently, could be seen in the ruins of a cowshed, a layer of brushwood between the rafters and the iron roofing sheets. This primitive insulating layer was a method commonly used in local farm buildings.

Crossing the water from a strong spring the path goes through a gate into what was Gotherington Wood. Apart from a few planted larches this wood has been cut down and is now a wasteland of willows, hazel, thorn and impenetrable brambles with the wild clematis or old man's beard covering almost everything. The path however is clear and leads to a gate marked by a wayfaring tree whose clusters of creamy white flowers of summer give berries first red, then black.

Past this gate the path is less distinct but leads across the rough uneven field towards Bushcombe Wood ahead. Sometimes this field with its hummocks and scattered thistles has a small herd of bullocks which may follow you with curiosity. The stile which gives into the dappled shade of the wood is in the upper part of the wall. This is a wood of overgrown coppice, mainly hazel and ash. Great chains of wild clematis hang down from the branches like the lianas of a tropical forest. In this wood, near the path, are some twayblade plants but I have never found the helleborine mentioned in the old book or the herb paris. Nevertheless Bushcombe Wood is a good example of what is called an ancient semi-natural woodland. Near the place where the path leaves is a small clearing which usually has a few tall burdock plants.

Crossing the stile out of the wood you can go down right over a wall and across a field to Bushcombe Lane, or to the left above the pines and above the buildings of the Little Slades to reach Longwood Common. This has not been grazed or burned for many years and is entirely covered with coarse grass and clumps of thorn and bramble.

There is a good view of the Cleeve Hill houses on the opposite hillside below Cleeve Cloud cliff with Thrift Wood to the right. This is a typical Cotswold view once used as the cover of an Ordnance Survey tourist map of the Cotswolds.

The road leads to the left back to Wickfield Lane past the barn of Longwood Farm and on the way there is a fine view southwards to Gloucester and the Forest of Dean hills.

2. A Walk in the Vale. About 4 miles (6.5km.)
Woodmancote to Gotherington and return along the lower slopes of Nottingham Hill.

An eminently rural place is Gotherington with its several considerable farm houses and farm yards, orchards and fowl-runs and old thatched or tile-roofed dwellings of shepherds and ploughmen and keepers of hens and bees.

> J. H. Garrett, *From a Cotswold Height.*

This walk leads from the Winchcombe road along the slopes of Nottingham and Holder's hills and back by a similar path a little lower down. Since it is in the clay country it is liable to be muddy.

From the car park on Stockwell Common Stockwell Lane leads steeply down past Emblem Cottage, once occupied by the jockey George Stevens and named after his winning mount in the 1863 Grand National. Just after the point where Post Office Lane joins there is a stile on the right leading to a green alley which comes out in a field with a low stone barn (grid ref. SO 982272). This is reputed to be the remaining part of a tobacco barn used for storing the crop when it was grown in the district. This trade was forcibly suppressed by the government in the seventeenth century as it competed too much with the trade of the American colonies.

The little stream running down the valley is crossed and we walk up through the thistly field where some of the great woolly thistles may be found, until we reach the traces of a green track. This is followed to the left through the hedge

towards the large house once called Mount Vernon, now The Round House, with its round tower.

Elm stumps, Gotherington, 1987.

The easiest way is to take the bridleway which runs below the grounds of the house to the lane and then, just before Stockwell Lane is reached, to the right taking a bridleway which soon runs between fences above the Apple Tree Inn to reach Bushcombe Lane. A more interesting way is to find the stile which leads to a path running just below the hanger wood above the grounds of the Round House and comes out on to an area with many bracken fronds and other plants of a more sandy, acid, soil. This path then runs between fences and reaches Bushcombe Lane beside Jasmine Cottage, a little above the other path. Between the points where these paths meet the lane, and on the opposite side, is the waymark for the next stage of the walk, over a stile near a house. It continues through what were in the old book picturesque apple orchards but have now been cleared and used for grazing small numbers of sheep and as 'pony paddocks'.

From around here is a good view of the towns of the vale. Nearby the tower of Bishop's Cleeve church rises above the buildings of that place now a small town rather than a village. Christchurch tower, Cheltenham, is the highest of the older buildings, the Eagle Star tower seems incongruous. Churchdown Hill leads the eye towards Gloucester where, if the light is right, the cathedral tower stands out.

The path goes towards the corner of a house called the Wynyards, then into a field showing good ridge and furrow patterns on the ground. These were made by the repeated use of a single furrow plough in the narrow individual strips in the common field, always turning the soil in the same direction. They have survived in many places where the fields have become pasture. The path then crosses three narrow strip fields which run up the hill. These were no doubt enclosed from the strips of individual farmers in the common field, probably about the end of the eighteenth century even though the enclosure award of Bishop's Cleeve did not take place till 1847. The path crosses three of the field boundaries by massive single-stone stiles of which there are several examples in this area but which are not often seen elsewhere.

The path runs below a large irrigation pond and enters the fields of the fruit farm on the south-west-facing slopes of the hill where they get maximum sun. Plastic irrigation hoses may be lying on the ground like enormous snakes. The flora which in summer has on this part of the walk been that of pasture and wayside now changes to the weeds of cultivation, like shepherd's purse, knot-grass, plantains and mayweed. The fruit farm has beds of strawberries, rasp-berries and other fruit, the rows of various ages, the young waiting to replace the old and less fruitful.

Keeping well above the old railway track the path goes through a couple of moist meadows where the bulbous buttercup grows in early summer and a few cowslips once common in the area can be found. In the last field before reaching Gotherington Manor Lane there is a line of a dozen white elm stumps now fast decaying, where a hedge once stood. Cut down in the 1970s after their death as a result of the Dutch elm disease epidemic of that time, they are a dramatic reminder of what we have lost. The ravages of this disease are caused by a particularly virulent form of the fungus which was imported in timber from America and spread by the elm bark beetle. As a result the tall English elm, once so characteristic of our countryside, has practically disappeared as a tree. They live on as suckers which are seen in many hedgerows but so far have not grown to full-sized trees and are still susceptible to the beetle and fungus. A new hazard is that modern mechanical flail hedgecutters are often operated so that no hedgerow trees survive, unlike the old hand hedge laying when standard trees would be selected and left to grow at intervals.

The path comes into a lane leading to Gotherington Manor Farm and the path up Nottingham Hill. In the grounds are several large old apple and pear trees, a pleasing sight when in bloom. Near them is a large square stone dovecote, the inhabitants of which would have been an addition to the food supply of the manor, though unwelcome to farmers.

Though today by no means the rural backwater described in the quotation from the old book, Gotherington is still a quiet place. Many of the old stone cottages remain, some with thatched roofs, more common in the vale than stone tiles, and some with timber framing. There is a pleasant development of houses with open-plan gardens along a new road. The village inn still has the unusual name of The Shutter. The place is quite rural enough to have many birds in summer, chiff-chaff, willow warbler, chaffinch, among others.

The return to Woodmancote from Gotherington Manor starts by taking the lane under the old railway and then at the corner turning into a large field where there is a stile and an iron gate (grid ref. SO 969293). This large field has been ploughed and the ridge and furrow patterns it showed have almost disappeared. Near an electricity pole there is a footpath sign and we take the path to the left which leads to a stile and a plank bridge. From there the path leads straight to the next stile and from there towards the railway bank and crosses it. After the railway the path leads through an orchard to the lower part of the fruit farm near some plastic-roofed buildings and yards. In the hedge just before they are reached is a good example of a wych elm shooting up from a stump. It too was probably affected by the elm disease, cut down and the new stems are springing up from the old base. Its leaves are larger and rougher than the English elm and the asymmetrical lobing of their bases where the stalk joins is easy to see. When I last passed this way, one early May, there was a good crop of the pale green winged fruits called samaras.

Past the farm buildings the path leads into a metalled lane, Butts Lane, which after passing two older and a number of modern houses reaches Bushcombe Lane at a point a little lower than where the path by which we came reaches it. We turn left and a little way along, at the corner, is a path which leads towards the Apple Tree Inn and the paths we started along.

Good views of Bishop's Cleeve church tower standing out in the flatness of the vale are obtained from Butts Lane and two footpaths lead to it. This is a convenient place to mention the village, now really a small town. Many of the old houses were pulled down when the new centre was built in the 1950s to accommodate the needs of the new housing estate. Scattered old houses, some of them half timbered, remain, and one or two were clearly originally of the 'hall' type, like the Old Farm at the end of Station Road.

The chief glory of the village however is the church, which has some of the finest Norman and Transitional features in the county. There are good examples of Norman snake-and-chevron carving on the west and south doors. The tower and the nave arches were rebuilt in the seventeenth century. At this time the nave arches were doubled in width. The great monument in the south aisle to Robert De la Bere of Southam, who died in 1636, and his wife, is characteristic of monumental art of the time, and hidden behind spiky wrought-iron railings. Squeezed up beside it is another, much earlier, effigy of a lady. Of the many other remarkable features of this church, looked after by a lively church community, may be mentioned the room over the porch used in the 1820s as a school room and with extraordinary wall paintings by the schoolmaster of that time. These include a tiger, a skeleton and an apocryphal battle scene with elephants.

On the main Evesham road is the old Rectory, a house dating from the thirteenth century and of original hall type but altered in the seventeenth century to give the 'Venetian' windows. Opposite is the remaining part of the tithe barn, now the village hall and beside it a stone cider press.

3. Langley Hill to Stanley Pontlarge and return from Gretton. 5 miles (8 km.)

The slope of the hill on which I stood, on that side called Stanley Hill, or Stanley Mount, sank down by billowy banks and mounds to Gretton and the road and railway that pass through that village.

J. H. Garrett, *From a Cotswold Height.*

This path explores Langley Hill north-west of Winchcombe and visits Stanley Pontlarge and Gretton on its northern side.

The Wychavon Way long distance footpath leaves Winchcombe by starting at the Corner Cupboard Inn (rid ref. SP 020281) going up Malthouse Lane and then by Harvey's Lane up Langley Hill.

In this walk we do not follow it where it leaves the lane going to the right, but continue straight on to Langley Hill Farm. From here the path continues northwestwards as a bridleway with good views across the valley of the Langley brook. To the right of Winchcombe the view goes up the Sudeley valley past the castle with its tower. On the other side of the Langley valley the long, bare, high plateau of Cleeve Common stretches with the cluster of radio masts near its centre. To the left at the edge of Humblebee Wood is the green mound of Belas Knap and the woods form a background to Corndean Hall.

To the right of the track, a field's breadth away, a line of trees marks the top of the little scarp of Langley Hill, facing north. This line curves round and reaches our track at a point where there is a gate. This is another of those remote Cotswold spots where there is a fine view over a pleasant, gently wild, foreground. The view shows Woolstone and Dixton Hills with Dixton Manor and the Malverns directly behind. To the right is the long line of Bredon with Alderton Hill, its village and green cultivated fields in front. Just below is an isolated cottage with a red tiled roof among the bushes. The track, which descends by a sunken way, bends to the right towards the attractively grouped buildings of Stanley Pontlarge Farm. On going down to them we find that some of the farm buildings have been converted to houses but the special features have been kept. On the other side is the large Victorian Manor Farm and an older stone house.

Opposite to these is the little church of Stanley Pontlarge. It is a surprise to find this Norman church, no larger than a small chapel, in this tiny hamlet. The south door has elaborate Norman carving but entrance is by the simpler north door. Inside the simplicity is striking, with a stone flagged floor, some ancient bench ends and very simple font. The fine Norman chancel arch is now distorted by movement of the ground. There are two fine mural tablets, one recording the happiness of a modern family for the privilege of living nearby.

One is brought back from medieval times by passing under the railway bridge. This carried the Cheltenham–Honeybourne line, opened in 1906 and closed for passengers in 1968. It is now being prepared for re-opening by

63

the Gloucestershire and Warwickshire Steam Railway Company as a restored steam railway.

From Alderton Hill looking towards Langley Hill and Cleeve Common.

There is a field path which leads from near the church to Gretton but it may be easier to walk the short distance along the road to the right. Gretton has a church of 1868 with a tall spire in a churchyard with pine trees. It was built by the philanthropy of Mrs Dent of Sudeley. There are some old houses but it is possible the oldest building is the base of the tower of the church of probably the fifteenth century. Round it are thatched cottages forming a group, possibly the original centre of the village.

We can return to Winchcombe over Langley Hill by a number of routes. The shortest and best marked is by taking the Wychavon Way starting in Duglinch Lane near the Bugatti Inn (grid ref. SP 008304). This is the local headquarters of the Bugatti Car Club which holds hill climb trials on Prescott hill several times a year.

The path leaves Duglinch Lane going left at the entrance to Gretton House and passes between hedges of Lawson's cypress shrubs. It then goes over a stile into what appears to be someone's lawn but the waymarks are clear beside the brook. At another stile it changes direction towards the corner of the large metal building ahead and then along the edge of a field to a ladder stile up a bank. From there it climbs up a slippery and wet field to a new track leading to the site of Warren Farm.

*From Nottingham
Hill northwards to
Toddington Church
and Meon Hill.*

Across this it goes up towards the woods of Langley Hill scarp and reaches
the ruins of Warren Lodge. These are quite extensive but now overgrown. It
would have been difficult for wheeled traffic to reach this isolated spot. From
there the path goes below the woods to a gate which gives onto a bridle way. A
little way along this to the right is an old quarry track which goes to the top of
Langley Hill. This area was once thought to be an ancient camp but is now
considered to be only the result of quarrying, as there is a cap of oolite stone on
the hilltop. From here there is a good view of Winchcombe and northwards to
Gretton and Alderton. Although there are many thorn trees in the hollows the
grass is kept short by cattle grazing.

Returning to the main bridle way it can be followed to Langley Farm or the
short cut taken across the field to Harvey's Lane down to Winchcombe.

An alternative is to leave Gretton by Greenway Lane, a little further along
the road to Winchcombe, a pleasant, sunken way which passes through a wooded
dingle with hart's tongue ferns, and the massive, green, mossy, fallen trunks of
old trees. There is a pleasant view of the village below and surrounding hills.
The track becomes steep and muddy but eventually reaches the bridleway which
going to the right reaches the hill top and Langley Farm.

Chapter Six

Over the Divide

The whole hillside, ranging from the valley's head to Salter's Hill is from here in
view and not so far off but that the details can be followed. All its numerous woodlands and trees showed magnificent on this autumn day, from the larch spinney by
the brook, whose green had turned to yellow, to the woods that extended along the
top and showed russet for the beeches with mingled shades of gold and red and
green for the other foliage.

J. H. Garrett, *From a Cotswold Height.*

A S WE HAVE SEEN most of the Cotswold streams flow eastwards towards
the Thames and only a few short ones flow westwards towards the
Severn or Avon. The sources of these are usually not far from the scarp
and the exact watershed is not everywhere easily defined. The valleys of the
south- and eastward-flowing Coln and the northward-flowing Beesmoor or
Sudeley brook, a tributary of the Isbourne are, however, well back from the edge
and the watershed between North Sea and Bristol Channel is clear. The area is
well worth exploring on foot with some beautiful views and interesting stone
villages.

The walk can be started from the southern end at the village of Whittington.
This lies a short distance from the A40 and Andoversford (grid ref. SP 015208).
It lies on the old road from Cheltenham and Charlton Kings towards the east.
The present line of the A40 and the connecting road to Whittington date only
from 1825. This connecting road passes the little church with Norman features
and great yews in the churchyard. Nearby is Whittington Court, the oldest part
of which is sixteenth-century on an older moated site. For some years until
recently it was the site of the Whittington Press, a hand operated press special-
ising in producing limited editions of beautifully printed books. It has now
moved to Herefordshire but retains the name.

Opposite the drive to the court is a path which crosses a field to the site of a
Roman villa and later of a medieval settlement, traces of which can still be seen
on the ground. Further east, by the abandoned railway, is the place where an
important Romano-British settlement existed, but which has left no traces
visible to the casual observer.

Past the court we go to the junction and turn right into the main street of
the village where many of the old stone houses are being modernised.

The road rises and passes a junction where a lane turns off leading northwards,
to the narrow part of Cleeve Common called West Down. This was Racecourse
Road at the time when races were held on the Common up to 1855, as described in

Sevenhampton Church.

chapter two. It linked the Common directly with the main road. We ignore this turning and take the road straight on dipping down to the Coln at Syreford.

The road crosses the river and soon after a track leads off northwards to the left opposite a bridleway to Andoversford (grid ref. SP 029204). Going well above the stream, this leads past two picturesque houses and soon enters a wood. The level track through this rather dark wood runs along a steep bank with the stream below. In January the entrance is marked by clumps of snowdrops escaped from a garden, and later on it has the characteristic Cotswold woodland flowers of lords and ladies, dog violet and twayblade. The trees are mostly beech and sycamore with some holly. In places a tree has fallen and been left, giving a primeval look. Towards the far side the deciduous trees are mixed with dark cypresses before the path goes through a gate and comes out into a field. The upper part of this has been planted in the modern manner with native deciduous trees—oak, ash, hazel—and their stems may be still protected by white plastic guards.

Keeping well above the brook the path becomes a bridleway leading into Sevenhampton village. This picturesque spot still has the ford for the road and a footbridge for pedestrians once common at the places where Cotswold roads crossed streams. Taking the path close to the brook, where, in summer, there is usually a cluster of the yellow monkey plant, we cross between two stone houses and climb up a steep bank to where Sevenhampton church tower comes into view seeming to grow higher as we approach it.

The path reaches a lane opposite the entrance to the churchyard. The scene here with the white flagpole to the left and the church with its little central tower is one of the best of Cotswold church views. The churchyard is like a garden, beautifully kept with garden flowers beside the path. The church itself has several features of interest. There is a tall narrow chancel arch which emphasises the difference in the widths of the nave and chancel. This caused a problem in building the central tower and there are internal flying buttresses which help support it. There is a good brass of John Camber of Worcester, wool merchant and the probable builder of the tower. The date of his death is 1497 and he is shown in a long robe with girdle and purse.

Part of the churchyard is bounded by the wall of Sevenhampton Manor, the upper part of which is ruined following a fire in the 1950s. A path leads from the lower churchyard into a field above the brook. When I passed this way many speckled black and white free-range hens, ducks and some geese shared the ground with a few sheep. The big stone house of Manor Farm is just above with a fine range of buildings both old and modern.

The path leads down to the stream, now quite small. Ahead is the red brick chimney with its stone top marking the site where a village brewery once stood. We cross the stream by a bridge and go along by a track between the houses of Brockhampton. The main lane is soon reached. To the left is the great pile of Brockhampton Park near the junction with the Syreford–Winchcombe road. This was the home of Fulwar Craven, a swashbuckling figure of early nine-teenth-century Cheltenham. Since his time the house has been rebuilt and has been offices for the Dowty engineering firm and is now divided up into apartments.

Brockhampton is about a third of the way to Winchcombe. The Craven Arms provides good refreshment and is the only inn on this walk. The route goes up the hill to the corner by the old chapel building where we turn left and go forward to the right-angled corner with an iron kissing gate in front of us. We go through this taking the footpath along the edge of the field. The land here is sometimes used for growing modern crops and I have seen the hillside misty blue in July from the flowers of linseed. Near here, too, I have found poppies growing at the edge of the field, the red and blue making an unusual contrast. Some of the next large fields, in one of which the Coln rises, seemed to have been allocated to 'set aside' when I was last there, with many wild plants like heart's-ease pansy, forget-me-not and scarlet pimpernel. The thistles were being cut, to stop them seeding. The path goes through this flat area and reaches the tarmacadamed road which is part of an ancient way coming off Cleeve Common, going up to Roel Gate and continuing eastwards towards the villages of the Windrush valley.

As a diversion one may walk up the hill to the right and see the small Roel camp on the left. Its shallow single ditch and mound do not quite complete an enclosure. A little further on the lane meets the Salt Way at the lonely crossroads of Roel Gate. Nearby is a memorial seat inscribed 'Arthur Edwin Boycott Pathologist Naturalist Friend 1877–1938'.

This must have been put up by the friends of Professor Boycott of University College Hospital, London. It is of interest to me, since we have a letter from him to my father thanking him for writing the book, which he says had greatly increased his interest in the area when on holiday. By one of the coincidences which those who collect old books know sometimes happen, I was looking at the books in a secondhand bookshop in Cirencester when I found a copy of *From a Cotswold Height* with Boycott's name on the fly-leaf and a letter from my father in reply to his pasted in.

The road eastward crosses another ancient north-south route, now a bridle-way, called Campden Lane, and further on at Roel Farm is the site of the deserted medieval village of Roel, mentioned in Domesday and with its own church, but depopulated by 1464. Campden Lane runs across the hill southward to Hawling where the people of Roel appear to have gone.

To return to our walk. The road, where we reached it from Brockhampton, marks fairly closely the watershed between Thames and Severn. Ahead lies the deep, steep-sided valley in which the northward-flowing Beesmoor Brook, the furthest source of the River Isbourne, rises. We can take the lane to Charlton Abbots or, more interestingly, the path which follows the road to Holt Farm with views down into the valley (grid ref. SP 036238).

The point at which the path leaves the private road was not well marked at the time of my visit, but it is near the young plantation. It descends the steep slope into the valley where there are three or four young horse chestnuts in protective cages and reaches the spring which has several trees near it. Near here too is a vast ancient pollarded oak, its trunk covered in massy woody excrescences, its branches rising from the same point and by their size showing that the last cutting had been done a long time ago. This method of tree management gave growth of timber out of the reach of grazing cattle but this tree—like so many others—has not been attended to for probably a century or more.

The definitive path leads to a deep and narrow holloway climbing to Charlton Abbots village which may be completely overgrown. In that case it is necessary to reach the road from the field by a gate. Charlton Abbots church is close by. This little church, in a delightful situation with its view down the wholly rural valley, was rebuilt in 1887. The churchyard contains a memorial to the heir of Brockhampton Park killed in the South African war, a rare memorial. There is also another to a local young man killed in an early aircraft accident.

The name Charlton Abbots indicates that this was a manor belonging to Winchcombe Abbey which is said to have had a leper hospital here. The garden retaining wall of the manor house is made of large ashlar stones which may be from an earlier building.

The lane leads northwards past the few houses of the village and ends at a gate where a field path begins. A line of thorns shows where the old track went. Here there is a fine view of the valley with Holt Farm and its varied woods on the opposite slope. The path climbs up to a stile just below Goldwell Farm Cottage. The buildings here, especially the great barn entrance and the farm as seen from the road, or near it, make a Cotswold scene well known to local artists.

I walked up to the road and northward along it towards Winchcombe, enjoying the views it gave of the valley until in about 200 or 300 yards I came to a bend where a gate barred the way to a rough track marked 'unsuitable for motors' (grid ref. SP 027252). This spot is one of my favourite viewpoints. The sloping hillside to the left with the dark mass of Humblebee Wood bordered by the road, the yellow track leading through the field to the edge of Little Humblebee ahead, the rough slopes, usually dotted with white sheep, leading down past ash and other trees to the valley bottom to the right, and on the other side the slope rising to the stone buildings of Sudeley Lodge, Sudeley Parks Farm and beyond them the isolated stone barn on the hill top, make a perfect scene especially late in the afternoon when the sun lights it from the west. Lower down the view opens out to Winchcombe and the Vale of Evesham. It must have

been the view from near here that the quotation at the head of this chapter *Winchcombe Church.*
describes and the essentials have changed little in over seventy years.

I took the track and passing by the lower edge of Little Humblebee Wood
came to Humblebee Cottages and a rough road leading down to Wadfield.
Across the road here is a short path which goes to a walled copse in which is a
small hut covering the scant remains of a Roman villa's tessellated pavement,
re-set in cement. This does at least show that the area has been a favoured site
for over 1600 years. Across the valley at Spoonley Wood is another, larger, villa.

The rough road leads down the hill, through a field of ripe corn at the time
of my visit, with views of the open vale, past the large farm of Wadfield—the
woad field. The house is a large Jacobean one with tall windows and elaborate
gateposts for the garden.

Below this the path leads through grassy fields in one of which stands another
massive oak at least 200 years old. Here the yellow stones of Sudeley Castle are
not far away and the partly ruined tower is clearly seen. The last field has a good
view of Winchcombe church unexpectedly high on its bank above the Isbourne,
its tower with the great gilded weathercock standing out. The field path joins
the metalled road near the entrance to Sudeley Park. Crossing the river this
comes into Vinyard Street with its pleasant houses close to the centre of
Winchcombe.

Sudeley Castle, the banqueting hall.

Sudeley Castle and gardens, open to visitors in the summer, can be reached from Vineyard Street by the road which passes the gatehouse and goes down a beech avenue to a bridge over the brook. A path to the right leads into the park and up the valley, but to enter the gardens it is necessary to follow the road round past the ticket kiosk to the garden shop. Then past the base of the square dungeon tower with its ruined top you turn the corner of the courtyard, one wall of which is formed by the ruined banqueting hall with its magnificent windows. Beyond that the queen's garden has been restored to re-create the appearance it might have had in Tudor times. The flower beds lie between two rows of double yew hedges. The remaining side is raised as a terrace looking out onto the park. Outside the area bounded by the yew hedges rises the chapel of St Mary, a Victorian restoration by Sir George Gilbert Scott. It contains the nineteenth-century white marble tomb of Katherine Seymour with a copy of the inscription on her original coffin.

To those with a sense of history Sudeley can be a magical place. It was visited by Richard III and the ruined windows we see today are probably his work. For a brief time in the sixteenth century it was the home of Katherine Seymour, the last wife of Henry VIII, after her marriage to Lord Seymour. It seems to have been a centre of Protestant thought where Miles Coverdale, a translator of the Bible, was chaplain, and Lady Jane Grey, later the five days' queen, stayed for a time.

Katherine gave birth to a daughter on 30 August 1548 and died on 5 September. Her husband, the unscrupulous and self-seeking Lord Seymour, is said not to have attended her funeral and was soon intriguing for the hand of the Princess Elizabeth and against his brother, the Lord Protector. It seems he richly deserved his execution six months later. The fate of the child is not known with certainty. Later Queen Elizabeth I visited Sudeley three times and in the Civil War Charles I came there after withdrawing from Gloucester and it changed hands four times, eventually being 'slighted' by the parliamentarians. In the eighteenth century it fell into ruin and was saved by the Dent family who acquired it in the mid-nineteenth century.

Although the romantic aspect of Sudeley owes much to Emma Dent's book *Annals of Winchcombe and Sudeley*, walking round the grounds today it is easy

to imagine oneself back in Tudor times when for a few months in 1548 it may have been the place where an almost royal court was held, and where it is said 120 gentlemen of the household and yeomen of the guard and others lived, and it was a centre of the reformed religion. Each summer Sudeley is the appropriate setting for a Tudor entertainment in costume or a re-enactment of a Civil War event which helps to re-create the atmosphere of those times.

Sudeley Castle, the gardens and chapel.

Part of the castle has been made into craft workshops and the interior contains many treasures, particularly the 'Tudor Portrait' of Henry VIII, his son, and his two daughters, contrasting the war-like Mary and her husband Phillip of Spain with the peaceful and prosperous Elizabeth. In the hall are relics of both sides in the Civil War: four huge leather blackjacks for beer, two with the arms of Charles I and two with Cromwell's.

Chapter Seven

Traces of the Middle Ages

[The pilgrim would go] onto a road purposely direct to Ford Hill and Farmcote, where he came suddenly into full view of the grey-golden Abbey far below, standing within its ample rectangular precinct wall, with its long leaded roofs, central tower and pinnacles, and the magnificent chevet of its buttressed choir chapels.

W. St Clair Baddeley, *A Cotswold Shrine* (1908).

THIS WALK takes us from the Anglo-Saxon borough of Winchcombe to the ruins of the monastery of Hailes Abbey, then up the scarp slope to the Iron Age Beckbury camp and to Campden Lane. Then past Stumps Cross down Coscombe valley to Wood Stanway and back to Winchcombe. About 8 miles (13 km.).

Winchcombe was an important centre in Anglo-Saxon times being capital of the Mercian sub-kingdom of the Hwicce. The surrounding country was named Wincelcombe-shire until the early eleventh century. At the Domesday record it was second only to Gloucester in the county and had about 150 burgesses. The Benedictine abbey was, as we have seen in the account of the legend of Huddlestone's Table in chapter four, established by King Kenulf in 798. Its most distinguished abbot was the last but one, Richard Kidderminster, who served Henry VIII as ambassador to the pope in 1512 before Henry's break with Rome. He died in 1531, well before the abbey was dissolved by order of his royal master in 1539. There were then only the abbot and seventeen monks and they were pensioned off. The buildings of the monastery lay behind the wall which runs along Abbey Terrace. The abbey church was declared superfluous and soon pulled down. The townspeople had their own church, built a century before, unlike Tewkesbury whose council bought the abbey when the monastery was dissolved.

Winchcombe church is one of the less elaborate of the Cotswold wool churches. There is no chancel arch, which gives a sense of spaciousness and enables the great east window, with its unusual nineteenth-century stained glass picture of Christ walking on the water, to be easily seen. Outside, the church is renowned for its grotesque gargoyles and great gilded weathercock.

The stone houses of Winchcombe have not changed much, but the town has spread outwards. The sixteenth-century half-timbered former George Inn which has a gallery in the courtyard and the initials R K for Richard Kidderminster carved over the doorway, has been altered and is now apartments.

The walk can begin just across the Isbourne bridge down Vineyard Street, where a footpath to the left starts which runs beside the river through fields giving unfamiliar views of the backs of the old Winchcombe houses along Hailes

Street. The path reaches the hamlet of Footbridge, so called because until the late nineteenth century the road to Broadway crossed the Isbourne by ford and footbridge, as with many other Cotswold streams. The way to Hailes follows the Cotswold Way to the right along Puck Pit Lane (grid ref. SP 029289). This, the 'hollow of the fairies', is one of the original pilgrims' ways to Hailes Abbey. The modern main road only dates from the turnpike era of the late eighteenth century. This lane, at first tarmac later stony, becoming a field path at a gate, leads directly towards Hailes. There are views of the wooded Cotswold slopes on the right and the low hill of the Warren, topped with tall trees on the left. Through a field with shallow ridge and furrow patterns, the track leads through a gate into a bridleway. This comes to a road which is followed to the right and soon a row of stone cottages, one called Pilgrim Cottage, is reached.

The path goes in front of the houses to a field in the middle of which is a stone structure which is the base of the old village cross. It then runs beneath the great chestnut trees and along the hedge which marks the present boundary of the abbey grounds. From here there is a very pleasant view of a short arcade of arches seen against the great trees across the cloister garth. The path reaches the road opposite the great yews at the entrance of Hailes churchyard. Before exploring the abbey ruins we should look at this little church, which has many unusual features.

The interior of Hailes church may seem damp and mouldy, as it is seldom used; but for the student of ecclesiastical history it is interesting for a number of reasons. First, like few other churches, it retains the puritan layout of the chancel with no altar rail but with panelling all round to which seats were fixed.

Hailes is also noted as one of the Gloucestershire churches with important pre-Reformation wall paintings and in the fourteenth century, when fresh, they must have been very colourful. On the north wall, seen on entering from the south door, is a gigantic figure of St Christopher, the patron saint of travellers. He is shown with his great staff crossing a stream. The Christ child is faintly visible on his shoulder. The splays of the windows in the chancel have figures of St Catherine on the north and St Margaret on the south. There are many other pictures of birds and mythical beasts and the coat of arms of the founder of Hailes Abbey.

The ordinary visitor, however, is most likely to be interested in the later painting of a quite secular hunting scene on the south wall of the nave. A huntsman with horn follows three lively greyhounds which are about to pounce upon a hare crouching under a small bush. From their expressions, the dogs have clearly seen the hare, whose cover seems quite inadequate. However there is a belief, told in an old *Flora and Fauna of Gloucestershire* (Witchell and Strugnell, 1892) that a hare could hide under a juniper bush and escape the hounds which were distracted by the juniper scent. Whatever is being shown here, and whatever its date, there is no doubt about the liveliness of the drawing.

Across the quiet road is the entrance to the ruins of Hailes Abbey, a National Trust property in the care of English Heritage. The little museum contains some excellent stone carvings, showing that Hailes was able to employ the best craftsmen.

Ruins of Hailes Abbey.

In contrast to Winchcombe Hailes was a Cistercian foundation, the monks wearing white habits, not the black of the Benedictines. The Cistercian order, originally following a more rigorous rule than the Benedictines, had relaxed by the time Hailes was flourishing and elaborate carvings and buildings were allowed.

The abbey was founded in 1245 following a vow made by Richard, Earl of Cornwall (later King of the Holy Roman Empire), as a result of being saved from shipwreck. He was a younger son of King John and brother of Henry III who gave him the manor of Hailes. The abbey was dedicated in 1251 in the presence of Richard, the king and queen and their son, later Edward I. They would have come along the way we have come, as would many of the pilgrims of later years when Hailes had become one of the great pilgrim shrines of England, and important enough to be mentioned in Chaucer's Canterbury Tales. The relic they came to see was the 'Holy Blood' which had been bought in Holland by Richard's son, and authenticated as the blood of Christ. It was, of course, only another example of the cult of superstitious relics which pervaded Europe in medieval times and was exposed at the Dissolution when it was declared to be no more than an 'unctuous gum'. It had been brought to Hailes in 1270 with great pomp and a special shrine built for it. The contributions of the pilgrims much enhanced the abbey funds. At the Dissolution Thomas Cromwell's commissioners, having closed Winchcombe, moved to Hailes and closed it on Christmas Eve 1539. The last abbot and twenty-one monks were pensioned off.

Of the church and shrine only the outline remains visible in the foundations. The best ruin is the set of three arches at the entrance to the chapter house from the cloister. Before the 1960s the ruins were enclosed in a sort of 'secret garden' of trees actually planted on the old walls. These had to be removed when excavation and renovation of the ruins were taking place. The chestnuts are still there, however, and make Hailes one of the most beautiful places on the Cotswold Way. The stone arches against the great trees, the quiet and peace of the place, make it a spot to escape temporarily from the problems of the modern world, as much today as the pilgrims did, in their own way, five or six centuries ago.

Our walk continues along the lane running towards the hills past the entrance to Hailes Fruit Farm. On the left is the ancient woodland of Hailes Wood. The stones of the track are in some places still clearly set on edge—a sure sign of an ancient way. It is, in fact, a way of ascending the Cotswold scarp as an alternative to the lane, usually considered the Salt Way, which diverges from it on the other side of the abbey. This was the route by which salt from Droitwich reached the Thames at Lechlade from where it was taken by boat to Oxford and London.

The sheltered valley with its fruit trees is a good place for birds and the wood, which is private, has many of the features of old woodland. Near its top the Cotswold Way leaves the track by a path over a stile on the left where there is a signpost. This is the way we will take—but before doing so it is worthwhile to make a diversion of about half a mile up the track to the hamlet of Farmcote, once probably a village itself. Here beside the lane is a farm, a big stone house, and a tiny yellow Cotswold stone church which is, in fact, only the nave of a larger building. The blocked chancel arch forms the east wall. This remote church in its grassy churchyard with views down the valley is another place where the pressures of the twentieth century seem far away.

To return to our main walk we take the Cotswold Way path over the stile signed 'Beckbury Camp 0.5 km' and follow it gently uphill across fields usually containing sheep. The second of these fields has two or three lynchets to the right of the path. These are broad shallow terraces made in medieval times to improve the ground for agriculture.

We follow the path towards a little scarp with a clump of tall old beeches on its top. The steep track passes their roots to reach the foot of the strange stone pillar, marked 'monument' on the map but the history and purpose of which no-one seems to know (grid ref. SP 063299). The trees are called Cromwell's Clump and the stone structure Cromwell's Seat, from the suggestion that Thomas Cromwell, the Hammer of the Monks, visited it at the time of the abbey's dissolution. Though there is good evidence that he did visit Hailes sometime before this, the structure is not Gothic but Classical; or, at least, not earlier than the mid-seventeenth century. It has a domed niche which suggests that it might have contained a statue or urn, and on another side there is a thick projecting stone shelf. The structure may have been put up by the Tracy family of Stanway, and may mark the limit of their estate or the boundary of Hailes and Stanway parishes which, in fact, runs down the rocky ridge towards the corner of Hailes Wood.

The place is a remote and gently wild one and a mild sense of achievement is gained by the steep little climb up to it. Many of the beeches are over-mature and decaying, and in their exposed position face the full force of the south-westerly gales. On a clear day the view stretches from the bare heights of Cleeve over Hailes Farm to Langley Hill. Then the hills of Woolstone and Alderton lead to Bredon with its varied fields and woods. Beyond, the Malverns close the view.

Cromwell's Clump.

Nearer, the houses of Winchcombe spread along the road to Greet, but at this distance do not yet spoil the rural scene. Down the little valley beside Hailes Wood are the houses and farms of Wood Stanway.

Here the scarp turns abruptly eastwards and we look north over a park-like area with scattered trees. The flat area is another promontory Iron Age camp, Beckbury Camp. Its perimeter is defined by the steep natural slopes and a single bank along the east and south sides.

Passing out of the camp over the bank our walk leads along the edge of the little north-facing scarp to the corner of the field by some fir trees, then round to the right to a copse, once a quarry, now a landfill site. There we join Campden Lane, another ancient north–south route, and follow the broad grass fringed track to the left. Away on the right in a slight hollow is a group of Cotswold farm buildings, Upper Coscombe Farm. In the 1939–45 war a school from Essex was evacuated there. The little church in the village of Cutsdean across the Stow road has a tablet commemorating the school's thanks for being able 'to worship there in peace and safety in the war years 1940–45'.

A short way along Campden Lane is a pond with four field walls meeting in the centre giving access for cattle from all four fields. Close by are several barns, and one of the buildings beside the lane is raised on staddle stones—a rare sight. The building appears to be made of metal sheets on a wooden frame with a rusty iron roof, probably a grain store. The staddle stones supporting it are used for their proper purpose, to prevent rodents climbing into the grain.

A fine avenue of old beeches runs from here along the wide grassy verge to the Stow road at Stumps Cross. Some have decayed but others have been planted to replace them. A field's breadth away to the left is a single line of beeches which edge the scarp and are a prominent feature from the vale below.

Building on staddle stones, Campden Lane, Coscombe.

Ridge and furrow patterns above Wood Stanway.

At Stumps Cross is the base of an ancient cross and the Cotswold Way turns left over a stile in the wall to a field. It soon reaches the steep slope and looks down the combe to Lower Coscombe Farm. From here there is a delightful view. In the distance the mound of Bredon Hill, the nearer Alderton and the dark wood on the side of Langley Hill are seen again. To the right the little valley separates off Stanway Hill with its wood concealing the main road to Stow. Across this is the pyramid marking the top of the slope where a cascade once led down to Stanway House. In the vale below are Wormington Grange and Toddington Manor in their parks. Walking down the slope we can appreciate the beautiful position of Coscombe, neatly sheltered from the north and east. No wonder it was a grange of Hailes, and the abbot's summer residence.

The fields below have a remarkably complex pattern of deep ridge and furrow through which the path goes down to Wood Stanway. This is another beautiful place, a quiet backwater embowered in great trees, already favoured in the seventeenth century as it has a number of stone houses of that time, larger than the usual Cotswold village house.

From here a number of paths lead. The Cotswold Way goes from Wood Stanway across the fields to Stanway and its great house. In the other direction it is a short distance along the road to Didbrook, the village to which the inhabitants of Hailes were moved when the abbey was built. Today it is interesting for its fifteenth-century church, which contains several of its seventeenth-century internal fittings. It is entered through a very small wicket door in the great west door. This shows what appear to be bullet holes, perhaps dating from the Civil War. The village has two cruck-beam half-timbered cottages. If we wish to return to Winchcombe there is a path through the fields from Didbrook back to Hailes.

Chapter Eight

The Outliers

Some portions of the view were blocked by a number of near hills that outlay the
Cotswold line like a group of green islands in the vale. Each of these island hills,
unlike its neighbour in form and lying in various positions apart from the others,
beautified the nearer distance after its own manner.

J. H. Garrett, *From a Cotswold Height.*

THE VALE COUNTRY seen from the scarp is varied by the outlying hills.
Once, long ago in geological time, they were part of the limestone ridge
but have been left isolated by erosion of the softer rocks towards the
east, leaving them standing as isolated remnants, each with a capping of more
resistant rocks.

A good view of these hills is the one obtained from the gate at the end of
Grinnell Lane on Nottingham Hill described in chapter five. The hills seen from
there look quite unspoilt and their varied appearance, with woods and fields,
invites exploration. All except Woolstone–Oxenton Hill have footpaths to or
near their summits and make interesting expeditions.

Dixton and Alderton Hills

We will start with Dixton Hill. There is no public footpath to the top but a
bridleway goes over the open ground below it.

On the road between Gotherington and Gretton and Winchcombe there is a
turning to the left to Alstone and Alderton, passing through the gap between
Woolstone and Dixton Hills. Coming from Gotherington after crossing over the
old railway, a lane to the right, opposite a farm, leads to the entrance to Dixton
Manor and becomes a bridleway, rejoining the Winchcombe road further on.
The car can be left at the beginning of this lane (grid ref. SO 983306).

Dixton Manor is a fine sixteenth-century Cotswold manor house with a
three-storied porch for the front door and four roof gables. Seen from the lane
across the pond with its,great trees and daffodils in spring, it seems the very
epitome of a country squire's house of that time. Built by John Hugeford, or
Higford, in 1555 it remained in that family until the early nineteenth century.

Its interest is greatly increased by the two great paintings now in Cheltenham
art galley. These, of the view from the hill just above the house, were made by
an unknown artist some time in the early eighteenth century and show the
numerous activities of a country estate in great detail. It is said that nowhere
else do we have so complete a picture of country life at that time.

The squire arrives in his coach and six to be greeted by his family. Sheep and cattle graze contentedly near the house. The mowers move synchronously in line across the hayfield. The girls gather up the hay into haycocks in the blocks of the meadow already mown. A group of Morris dancers disport themselves, ribbons flying. Carts are carrying the hay harvest away. One picture shows the enclosed fields near Dixton, the other the open field towards the south-west. From the bridleway we can see the background of the scene practically unchanged since that time. Dixton Manor is obscured by trees, but many other features can be identified. Particularly is this the case with the small farm on Pardon Hill opposite. The slope of the hill agrees with the picture. In one direction the road goes towards Winchcombe as in the picture. In the other direction, if the day is clear, we can see Gloucester Cathedral, its size emphasised in the picture, and the characteristic shapes of the Sugar Loaf and other Welsh hills, identifiable in the painting.

Looking south from Alderton Hill to Dixton and Woolstone Hills.

Returning to the car we continue along the lane leading between Dixton and Woolstone hills passing Alstone, a hamlet with a church with features from Norman to seventeenth-century times and some half-timbered houses. The road joins the main Tewkesbury–Stow road and we turn right. A little way along there is a lane to the left leading to the farm of Little Washbourne. A short way down this is the little church of this hamlet. It lies in a small plot of ground, beautified by daffodils in spring. It is a redundant but still consecrated church

From Dixton Hill towards Nottingham Hill.

The same view in the eighteenth-century painting of Dixton Manor in Cheltenham Art Gallery.

and is practically unchanged since the eighteenth century. Its furnishings and atmosphere are of that time, with a two-decker pulpit and old box pews.

The next turning to the left on the main road goes to Alderton, under its hill. Like so many villages which have grown in size over the last thirty to forty years, with many new houses and bungalows, it has changed in character. Most of the old inhabitants moved away finding more employment and less expensive houses in nearby towns. There were once five shops, now none.

The walk over Alderton Hill to Dumbleton can be made by taking the bridleway from the western end of the village or from the lane going towards the Stow road to the east. This is the way that will be described.

At a sharp corner on this road a track leads off to Frampton Farm (grid ref. SP 011329). Here is an ash tree with a metal plate commemorating the time between 1942–44 when the area was full of hutted camps for the US Army's ordnance depot. The plate was put up by former US Army sergeant, Ross Jones, on a return visit in 1988 to commemorate his happy association with the local people during the war.

The walk up the track leads past the farm with its large walnut trees and becomes a footpath crossing a meadow and then begins to climb the hill beside a wood. This is part of the Wychavon Way long distance path from Winchcombe to Holt Fleet on the upper Severn above Worcester. The rough ground of the little valley is pleasantly varied on its further side in late summer by a clump of the pink flowers of the tall rosebay. At the top where the path joins another is a good view back towards Dixton and Nottingham hills topped by the higher ground of Cleeve Common. The path turns left and goes along level ground between the trees. After passing through these rather sombre woods we emerge into an open cornfield with the buildings of Dumbleton Hill Farm on the other side. Near the farm is a delightful view of the slopes of Bredon Hill with the village of Ashton under Hill nestling at its foot and the little vale of the Carrant Brook in front.

The Wychavon Way is left behind here and our path, now a private road, descends through a park-like shallow valley towards Dumbleton village. On the right is Alderton Hill with its wooded summit lying next to the Warren, a bare hill of different geology. Here the change from lower to upper Lias with some marlstone gives a sandy ground with a rabbit warren and a different flora in which gorse is prominent. Down this pleasant park-like valley there are views of the garden of Dumbleton Hall with its lake, cedars and clipped hedges. The great house of Dumbleton, in the mock-Tudor style of the 1830s, is remarkable for its many windows and elaborate chimneys.

Dumbleton village has an interesting church with early Norman features. Looking round the outside you can see the projecting stones of the Norman corbel table just below the eaves. They are carved with grotesque heads, some animals, others difficult to make out. The tympanum over the north door has a rather crudely carved head eating a trailing vine. This may be an example of a 'green man', a fertility symbol surviving from pre-Christian times.

In the church is the coloured seventeenth-century monument to Sir Charles Percy and his wife kneeling opposite one another, with their only child who died in infancy represented chrysalis-like in swaddling clothes below.

Sir Charles was of the great Scottish border family of the Percys and third son of the Earl of Northumberland. His connection with Dumbleton was through his wife, who inherited the estate in the late sixteenth century. As recorded on this monument, his claim to fame was that—no doubt because of his knowledge of the Border country—he was chosen to accompany Thomas Somerset as one of the messengers who took the news of Elizabeth I's death to King James in Edinburgh after he had been proclaimed king in London.

From Langley Hill north towards Stanley Pontlarge and Alderton Village and Hill.

These two official messengers arrived several days after the news had been brought unofficially by Sir Thomas Carey, another courtier who depended on royal patronage for his position. The story of Carey's ride from Richmond Palace to Edinburgh in two and a half days, where he arrived 'beblooded by great bruises' sustained in falls from his horse, is a remarkable story in the annals of travel. Like Percy of a Border family, he had already ingratiated himself with King James. Immediately on hearing of the queen's death early in the morning of 24 March 1603, he tried to obtain the Privy Council's permission to act as messenger to Edinburgh but was refused. He evaded the guards and set off regardless. He had already prepared the way by having horses available at pre-arranged points. He stopped the first night at Doncaster, 160 miles from Richmond, and the next at his own house at Widdington, Northumberland. He reached Edinburgh late the next day, having had to slow down because of his falls, but still three days before the arrival of Percy and Somerset.

Dumbleton village contains several interesting old houses. It was clearly closely linked with the life of the great house and its estate. The Victorian Gothic drinking fountain, which seems so incongruous to us, was put up by the friends of Edward Holland of Dumbleton Hall and provided what, at the time, was no doubt considered a great benefit to the village—a source of piped water. The great house is now a holiday centre for post and telecommunication workers, and the large stables have been converted into flats.

Bredon Hill

The largest, highest and most interesting of the outliers is Bredon. Its top of Inferior Oolite rises to 299 metres or 980 feet. It is included in the Cotswold Area of Outstanding Natural Beauty and a part of its south-west slopes is designated as a Site of Special Scientific Interest. It is a prominent feature from many places in the vale and, especially when cloud-capped, is well known to local people as a weather indicator in the rhyme

> When Bredon Hill puts on his hat,
> Men of the Vale look out for that.
> When Bredon Hill shines fair and clear,
> Men of the Vale you have naught to fear.

There are several ways to the top. Probably the shortest from a place where cars can be left—though there is no proper parking place—is from the point where the tarmac ceases on the lane above Westmancote hamlet on the south-west slope (grid ref. so 946381) and this will be described. The length of this walk is about four miles (6.5 km.) and takes a leisurely two hours. There are, however, other routes of equal or greater interest. These include from Elmley Castle, from Overbury through the park, and up the steep old road from Woollas Hall on the west side.

The lane which comes from Bredon village to Westmancote ascends between the stone cottages where no doubt quarrymen lived. Past the tarmac it becomes a dusty track which originally led to quarries further up the hill, and goes along the edge of a field where the hedge parsley and burnet saxifrage—small umbelliferous plants—are to be seen in July.

Turning to the left at the top of the field the path goes to a gate and then along the top edge of the scarp wood of beech and ash. At this place the King and Queen Stones can be seen below at the edge of the open wood. There are, in fact, four stones, upright irregular masses of oolitic rock. They have been known to local people for centuries. It was here that the court leet of the manor of Bredon was held annually until about 1830 and the stones were whitewashed for the occasion. Passing along the top of the open beech and ash woodland, the path goes along the edge with a cultivated field to the right and the steep slope of rough grassland to the left. This would once have been closely grazed, but is now a picturesque wild area with many elder and bramble bushes. A few sheep may be grazing it and in the evening one may be fortunate enough to see some fallow deer. In this rough area are the yellow wild parsnip and scattered plants of the tall ploughman's spikenard. Their stiff and rather sticky, hairy stems and reddish-yellow clusters of compact small composite flowers are characteristic. From about here too you can get the first of the great views from this hill. The Vale of Avon lies below with the thin silvery line of the river seen here and there winding along beneath its willows. It is crossed near Bredon village by the M5 motorway whose constant roar cannot be avoided, though rather muted at this distance. There is a good view of the old stone bridge at Eckington, an earlier crossing place. Opposite across the vale Great Malvern clings to its hillside.

*King and Queen
Stones, Bredon Hill.*

The path goes on, leaving the edge, going beside an ash wood and then enters an open grove of beech and sycamore trees near the edge again. Soon it is joined by an ancient winding holloway which comes up from Woollas Hall. This early seventeenth-century great house has a three-storey porch, like Dixton. It was built by John Hanford and remained in the possession of the same family until this century. It is now divided up into apartments.

We go along the edge of a field and through more trees and suddenly see Bredon Hill tower just ahead. It is then a short scramble up the double ramparts of the fort and through the ditch to reach the flat top of the hill.

The ancient camp, called Kemerton or Bredon Hill camp, is one of the Iron Age chain mentioned in describing the example on Cleeve Hill. Its walls enclose about ten acres, cutting off an area bounded on the north and west by the steep scarp. It was excavated in the 1930s and evidence of a great battle found, with the bones of sixty-four dismembered bodies scattered unburied in the ditches. This occurred in the early part of the first century AD and probably ended the occupation of the site.

The stumpy tower, called Parsons' Folly from Mr Parsons of Kemerton who built it in the late eighteenth century, is said to raise the height to 1000 ft. It is now used to carry aerials for radio communications. Just below is the large irregular Oolitic mass called the Banbury or Bambury Stone. There are several stones, the two larger ones full of shallow holes from weathering and with a small space between them.

It is for the view that Bredon is justly famed as it extends in all directions and looking around at the varied scene one sees the aptness of Houseman's words 'coloured counties' when he described the scene in his *In Summer Time on Bredon*. From here Cleeve and Nottingham hills are seen end-on and appear foreshortened. The blue line of the Cotswolds runs behind Churchdown and Robin's Wood hills to where it turns westward in the promontory of Stinch-

Bambury Stones and Bredon Tower.

combe Hill. Across the Vale the Forest of Dean hills, with May Hill and its prominent clump of trees, continue the horizon to the Welsh hills and then the Malverns. These are much nearer to us from here than from the Cotswolds and also appear rather foreshortened. To the north the vale stretches to the rounded hump of the Wrekin, and nearer at hand the Avon flows past Pershore, easily distinguished by the green copper roof of its abbey tower. Tewkesbury and Worcester are visible, but Evesham is further round, visible by walking along the top to the east. The colourful vale in the foreground shows Great Comberton and other villages. The flat top of the hill with its great views and peacefulness due to its distance from any motor traffic, and its ancient banks and ditch with the steep north slope, make Bredon a very pleasant place on a summer's day.

The return to Westmancote can be made by walking along the wall above the edge, past a large stone stile, where a footpath comes up from Great Comberton, to a small pine clump, and then taking the bridleway to the right, southwards. This leads across three fields until there appears a path to the right leading to the remains of Sundial Farm. This is now only a restored barn with a new sundial on it, dated 1992. From there the path goes along a track beneath a line of ash trees. Where these cease at a stone gate post, it continues along a line of thorn trees well above the valley bottom towards the corner of the wood seen ahead which fills an old quarry. From there the path goes over a stile and is clear to the bridleway you started on.

An alternative descent, especially if a car has been left at Elmley Castle, is to go through the gate at the pine-tree clump mentioned above and follow the path which leads down to Elmley Castle. This goes down a rough grassy valley between two woods to the track which leads to that village.

Elmley is perhaps the most attractive of the Bredon Hill villages, which are considered some of the best examples of what is often thought of as the

86

characteristic English village—some thatched buildings, some half-timbering, some stone, cottage gardens full of flowers, an ancient inn, an interesting church.

Elmley Castle's castle, once the seat of the Beauchamps, was on the hillside a little way from the village. The wide village street has the Queen's Head Inn with a sign commemorating Elizabeth I's visit to the place on one of her tours around the country.

The most interesting feature is the church and its monuments in the north transept, which are among the best in England. The great early seventeenth-century monument with three recumbent figures is for members of the Savage family of Elmley. It is remarkable for the marvellously detailed carving of the clothes of all the figures. The man on the right is Sir William Savage, who died in 1616. He has a stiff ruff. Next is his son Sir Giles, who died in 1631 and has a soft ruff, long curly hair and a pointed beard. Next to him is his wife Catherine, who died forty years later, in 1671. She is in a long gown and holds a baby, elaborately dressed in cap, little ruff and long-clothes fastened with a gilded girdle. This baby is said to have been born after the death of Sir Giles and presumably died in infancy. The feet of the two men rest on lions with tails curled over their backs. At Catherine's feet is the head of a stag with a real crossbow bolt through the neck. Below are four children, the eldest boy on the left with sword and spurs, his hand on his heart, perhaps taking a vow. He fought actively for King Charles and was heavily fined for it.

On the wall opposite is a very different monument, the Baroque style half-reclining effigy of the first Earl of Coventry of nearby Croome Court. He is shown as a very pompous nobleman with wig and enormous cuffs. It was intended for the church of Croome d'Abitot where the Coventry family were usually buried and which is full of their elaborate tombs, but the earl's son disapproved of his father's second marriage and refused to allow it to be put up there.

In the churchyard is the tall pillar of a very curious sundial with eight faces, said to be able to tell the time in all parts of the Old World, but this seems most unlikely.

The other villages around Bredon Hill are worth visiting for their rural setting. Little Comberton has the fine half-timbered Nash's Farm and a stone dovecote.

The largest is Ashton under Hill which has some recent development and the main schools. Grafton, on the other hand, is a hamlet of little altered, scattered, stone and black-and-white farm houses on the hillside. Beckford is famous for its silk printing works where high quality hand crafted work is produced. The village must have been partly rebuilt or enlarged in the nine-teenth century, as there are several red-brick cottages. The south door of the church has an unusual carved Norman tympanum with a cross and an eye and a goose-like bird above, and below two animals with long horns and ears.

Overbury, another large village, has the fine eighteenth-century Overbury Court and several attractive stone and half-timbered houses. It is interesting to note the differences between the old half-timbering and the large Black and White Stores which is Victorian.

Most of these villages have a mixture of stone and brick, tiles and thatch, and can be thought of as showing the change from Cotswold to Vale type of house.

Chapter Nine

A North Cotswold Drive

The long, shallow valleys, the woody slopes, the complex of ridges converging and
diverging and vanishing into the sky, the composed though infinitely varied plateau, the landscape that to the eye touches the horizon at all points but always
across its own high level—these are the wolds.

H. J. Massingham, *Cotswold Country* (1937).

COTSWOLD SCENERY is characteristic both in its details and its general
extent: detailed in the features of buildings and their arrangement one
to another; general in the sweep of open hills, woodland, field walls and
farm buildings in the landscape. The scenery we have been describing so far has
been the country near the western scarp, and wherever we have gone we have
always returned to be dominated by that feature and its view. It is time to
discover that the Cotswolds have much of interest in what might be called their
'interior', away from the edge. Although the details of this country are best
appreciated by going through it at a walking pace, and there are many footpaths
and bridleways enabling you to see it in that way, for many people the only
practical way is to explore by car, so this chapter describes a trip through some
of the most interesting parts of the North Cotswolds. The emphasis has been
placed on the less well known and less spoilt places which motor coaches find
difficult to reach, though some very well known places are included. The trip
is about sixty miles long and can be completed in half a day, though all the
features of the area could not be properly appreciated in that time. To make a
tour of reasonable length, some interesting places have been left out for no other
reason than that they lie slightly off the main route. The places visited include
some well known for various reasons, and some not so well known, but which
have interesting features of history or scenery.

Though largely a personal choice, the route covers a fairly representative area
of North Cotswold scenery. Not included are some of the villages between the
Windrush and the Evenlode valleys, the hills to the east, including the Roll-
rights, and the country north and east of Chipping Campden. All these contain
places well worth visiting, but are too far flung to include in a single drive which
gives time to appreciate them.

We start by passing through Winchcombe which has already been briefly
described. Past the market place and Abbey Terrace we take the steep narrow
road, Castle Street, turning right when coming from the south at the corner of
the White Hart Inn and before the large black-and-white building, the George,
formerly a hotel but now apartments. The road descends steeply to the Isbourne
bridge. It then widens past the yellow stone gatehouse of Sudeley Castle, now

Guiting Power village.

used only as an exit and goes up Sudeley Hill. Up the hill and keeping to the main road where there is a fork we come to the edge of Guiting Wood. The spot is marked by a great beech and is near where the old Campden Lane crosses, though here it is not very obvious. This is one of the largest pieces of semi-natural woodland in this part of Gloucestershire and has been wooded since prehistoric times. Of course its nature has been altered by being managed and replanted. The road goes along the edge of the wood for some distance then dips to a valley where the road from Roel joins on the right. It then climbs up and with a view of the stone buildings of a large farm in a valley to the left with hills behind, it soon reaches the village of Guiting Power. This attractive place takes its name from the Norman family of Poer who held the manor and has nothing to do with water power, though Guiting is probably the ancient name of the upper River Windrush. The village has two small greens, one with a large horse chestnut tree, the other with a war memorial cross setting off the stone cottages.

We take a small road on the right at the second green. A side road from this leads to the village hall and church. Guiting and neighbourhood are very enterprising and have a small musical festival here in the summer. The church, of yellow stone, was drastically altered in the nineteenth century. The entrance is, unusually, by a Norman door now placed in the end of the south transept. Recently an excavation has been made in the open ground to the north of the church and the foundations of a Saxon church found.

The road to Naunton leads across an open field and forks sharply left to pass the entrance of Guiting nature reserve. This reserve has been made around three pools, created earlier this century for sporting purposes by damming a small tributary of the Windrush. It is a haven for water-loving plants and birds and there is a bank of open woodland above. The road climbs up to a house and group of stone farm buildings, passing on the way a gate on the left leading into woodland. This is the site of the Stone Pipe Quarry works started early in the nineteenth century. The story of the supply of stone water pipes to Manchester around 1810 is an extraordinary one of gullibility and naiveté on the part of many people. Even the famous civil engineer, Thomas Telford, seems to have been taken in for a time. The company set up a works here to drill oolite blocks into pipes. These were taken to Tewkesbury and travelled to Manchester on the river and canal system. At one time it was proposed to build a horse tramway to take the pipes to Tewkesbury. A lot of pipes were ordered by Manchester before it was realised that, apart from any difficulties with joints, they were porous and could not retain water under pressure. The site, now in woodland, was excavated in the 1980s. It is possible to find some of the cylindrical cores bored out of the blocks in the walls nearby.

We go past Tally-ho Farm and join the main Gloucester–Stow road, the B4068, at the Fox Hill Inn. Turning left we soon come to a cross roads where there is a large house, once the Naunton Inn. Here we fork left down to Naunton village. This is the original old village road, the 'by-pass' along the ridge being a turnpike road constructed to make travel easier in 1755.

The village of Naunton on Cotswold, to give it its full old title, lies pleasantly along the Windrush. Its church is the first feature of interest. The tower is very unusual in having two sundials painted on its corner, facing south and west. The

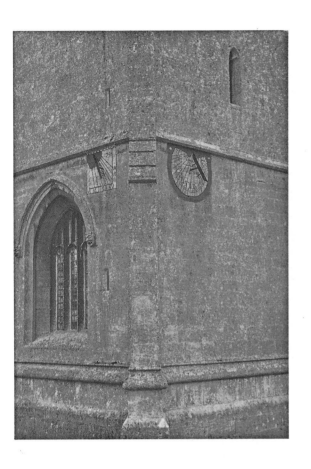

Naunton sundials.

west-facing one is in shadow till after mid-day and is marked with the hours from XI to VIII, the south wall one from V to IV. Inside the church, the best feature is the stone pulpit finely carved about 1400. Of more human interest is the wooden battle-field cross fixed to the wall commemorating a soldier killed in France in the First World War.

The village is pleasant to walk through, across the Windrush bridge and up the hill. On the right is the Baptist Chapel and its graveyard on a steep slope above the river. Further on, a rough road leads past a stone dovecote to a footbridge and a path which runs back towards the church. This makes a pleasant walk with a view of the village on the hillside.

The road through the village passes the Black Horse Inn, goes along the valley and meets the main road again at Harford Bridge. Opposite are two roads and it is the narrow left-hand one we have to take. This leads steeply up Harford Hill and then runs along the top of the wold with views down to the Windrush deep in its valley. Up here there is a view eastwards to the hills separating Windrush and Evenlode, with the radio mast marking Iccomb Hill, once the site of a tower. Turning right on reaching the Burton–Broadway road we soon turn left onto the road for Upper Slaughter. The name of this village and its sister, Lower Slaughter, has nothing to do with a battle, meaning only a muddy place or mire, like Slough.

These two villages with their curious name are widely known as characteristic of the Cotswolds. Upper Slaughter is neatly built on the steep bank above the Eyebrook and the churchyard gives a good viewpoint. Just below it is an oak on a sloping green overlooking the ford and footbridge with cottages nearby. The church itself is mainly of interest for the pointed Transitional Norman arches on typical Norman carved capitals, and for the elaborate Victorian Gothic tomb of the Rev. William Witts, rector here in the mid-nineteenth century, and whose diaries from 1820 to 1852 have been edited by David Verey and published in 1978. They give an interesting account of the life of an active country parson of the time, his meetings with many well known people, his journeys to Gloucester and Cheltenham and developments in the countryside.

To reach Lower Slaughter by road across the brook you have to drive up Copse Hill and then down to the village. After passing some new houses you reach the church corner and the road widens under some trees. This village has

one of the most photographed Cotswold scenes. To reach it you walk up the *Upper Slaughter ford.*
river past the Westbourne Court Hotel. The river here is crossed by several
footbridges and ahead is the turning mill wheel and chimney of what was the
village mill. The red brick chimney, an addition of the mid-nineteenth century
put in to supplement the water power with steam, reflected in the water, makes
here for once a pleasing contrast with the stone buildings. A mill was recorded
here in Domesday Book and corn was ground until the 1940s.

The Slaughters are one of the places best explored on foot and there is a very
pleasant walk up the Eye Brook from Lower Slaughter to the upper village and
to the Stow road at Eyeford. This starts near the mill. The village houses
have been completely restored and the attractions of the area have brought
many visitors who are accommodated in the three or four hotels converted
from large houses.

We take the lane from Lower Slaughter which leads to the Fosse Way, the
Roman road linking Exeter, Leicester and Lincoln, and forming at the time it
was built, about 45 AD, the boundary of occupied Roman territory. Just to the
east lies Bourton on the Water, perhaps the most visited of all the Cotswold
towns and villages. Its stream side walks, linked by low bridges across the river,
its model village and its bird gardens no doubt bring pleasure to many, but on
this tour we are concerned with the less well known places and will go up the
Fosse Way to Stow on the Wold. This, at 230 metres (700 feet) is the highest

Lower Slaughter mill.

town on the Cotswolds. At the junction of six roads it is a great communication centre, recognised by the Abbot of Evesham who granted a charter for a market in 1107. A great sheep fair was held in the wide market place along the Fosse. Today there is still a horse fair twice a year, in May and October. Horse dealers and breeders come from as far away as Wales to sell horses, mainly hunters and ponies, and there is a great gathering of travelling people and caravans. Stow is on a road to London and played a part in the Civil War. The battle fought there in March 1646 when the royalists were defeated was one of the last of the war. The prisoners were shut up in the church, which suffered damage.

Today Stow is mainly a town of hotels and antique shops. The Victorian St Edward's Hall on an island site in the wide market place is the town's cultural centre.

Leaving the town along the Oxford road we take the road towards Chipping Norton, the A436. This by-passes the villages of Upper and Lower Oddington which lie a little above it. We turn sharply right for the lower village and soon come into the narrow street of stone cottages and turn left down a lane for the old church. It is surprising to think that this place, now so obscure down a dead end road, was once a residence of the archbishops of York and was visited by royalty in the thirteenth century. King Henry III is recorded as coming here on journeys between his manor at Woodstock and Evesham and other places. He arranged for oaks to be sent to build the stables, and there must have been quite an establishment here. The road past the church was once a through-way to the south but is now only a bridleway. Later the place was considered unhealthy and the people moved to higher ground where the cottages are now.

The church is noted for having one of the best medieval wall paintings in the county. The original church, now the south aisle, was enlarged when the place became important, by building a new church on the north side of the old one. The north wall was built without windows and was decorated with a great 'Doom' painting; a Day of Judgement scene like the one in the great west window of Fairford church, and a frequent medieval theme. Much of the picture has inevitably faded since it was discovered hidden under whitewash in 1913 but much can be made out with the aid of the description in the church. Christ and His apostles, each with a halo, supervise the Day of Judgement. The lost souls are being taken away to hell by devils on the right, the saved souls are going into the heavenly city on the left. They are shown being helped by white-winged angels to climb the walls of a brick castle. This seems strange to us who are only too familiar with brick buildings, but can perhaps be explained by the fact that at the time this picture was made, in the late fourteenth century, brick was only just coming into use and was considered a new and desirable building material. Some of the first brick buildings were, in fact, in the Arch-bishop of York's domains in south Yorkshire, from where the artist may have come.

Returning to the main road we turn right to cross the River Evenlode and the main Oxford–Worcester railway and take the turning for Adlestrop, passing along the edge of the park. This place, with the strange name, has the chance distinction of being commemorated in a well known poem. The poet Edward Thomas was travelling in a train which stopped there one day in June 1911. The poem he wrote is very evocative for those who have experienced the great silence which descended when a steam train stopped unexpectedly at a deserted wayside station. It would be broken only by small sounds, the occasional word, or by birdsong outside, exactly as described in the poem.

Edward Thomas was killed on the western front in 1917 and the station no longer exists, but the fame or notoriety bestowed on Adlestrop persists. The station nameboard was fortunately saved and, with a seat, has been put up on the little green under a great oak. Perhaps the most remarkable thing is that the poem and the atmosphere of this quiet place with its yellow stone and thatch cottages under its wooded hillside has inspired others to write about it too.

Returning to the main A436 we go up the hill to the left, the road edged with great beech trees, until we reach a minor cross roads where the sign shows Chastleton to the left. Going along the hill top this road passes on the right a circle of trees which mark the place of an Iron Age hillfort or settlement. The road descends with a nice view of the vale ahead until round a bend we come to Chastleton House and church. Their grey-brown lichened stone seems to match exactly, but the house completely dwarfs the church in size. However, the interior of the church is larger than seems possible from the outside. The great house here was built about 1602 by Walter Jones, a wool merchant of Witney. Of all great houses it is one of the least altered from its original form, and even the furnishings are little changed. Its main features are the great hall and the long gallery with plasterwork ceiling. Recently acquired by the National Trust, it is at present being restored and is not yet open to the public.

The most interesting fact about Chastleton is that it was the scene of one of the most romantic stories of the Civil War. William Jones was fighting for his king at Worcester on 3 September 1651 and after the disaster of that defeat galloped homewards. It is very likely that he came by the 'Great Road' from Worcester which passes within a mile of Chastleton. He knew he was being closely pursued, as all the men of the parliamentary army were looking for the king and other fugitives. Arriving home, he gave his horse to a groom in the stables and dashed inside, where his wife concealed him in the secret room which is reached off one of the upper-floor rooms. The parliamentary soldiers soon arrived and demanded to search the house. Their suspicions were confirmed by finding a sweating horse in the stables, but they did not find the secret hiding place. They decided to stay the night, occupying the room through which it was necessary to pass to reach the secret chamber. Mrs Jones liberally supplied them with meat and drink laced with laudanum, which caused them to sleep heavily. While they were snoring she passed through the room and led her husband out. He took the parliamentary commander's horse and escaped. One can imagine the altercation the next morning, and Mrs Jones was lucky to escape imprisonment, but perhaps the roundheads felt very silly at losing their quarry.

From Chaseleton we drive to the Chipping Norton–Morton in Marsh–Worcester road, the A44. This passes the Four Shire Stone. This classical eighteenth-century low tower or column marked the spot where the boundaries of Gloucestershire, Warwickshire, Oxfordshire and Worcestershire met and the spot is said to have originally been marked with four Saxon stones. This was only possible by there being a separate enclave of Worcestershire around Blockley which extended to this spot but was brought into Gloucestershire in 1931.

Past the entrance to the Fire Service College on an old wartime airfield, we enter Moreton in Marsh. The 'marsh' part of the name was originally Henmarsh, a marsh frequented by wild birds. This is the more accepted derivation, rather than the one suggesting it is related to its nearness to the marches or boundaries of Gloucestershire.

Moreton has similarities to and differences from its near neighbour on the Fosse Way, Stow on the Wold. We have seen that Stow has its large open market place in the centre, and Moreton has an even larger one. There seems to be a greater variety of shops here than at Stow. Moreton, like Stow, did not exist in Saxon times and was established in 1226 by the Abbey of Westminster which held the manor of Bourton on the Hill nearby. It is the point where the old road from London and Oxford to Worcester crosses the Fosse Way. Like Stow the market place has an island building, in this case the Redesdale Market Hall. The oldest building is the Curfew Tower of the sixteenth century, still with its bell.

We leave Moreton along the Broadway road. This passes the entrance to the driveway leading to Batsford Park and Arboretum. A very pleasant hour can be spent here walking under the great trees near the house. There are many interesting varieties, especially magnolias in spring and Japanese maples in autumn. The park contains a herd of deer often seen from the drive. Opposite the entrance to Batsford is the drive to Sezincote. This remarkable house was built by Sir Charles Cockcroft on his return from India in 1805. It is in the Indian Moghul style with an onion dome, and precedes the better known Brighton Pavilion by ten years. It is open to the public on certain days in summer. Soon after this the main road starts to climb by the narrow road through Bourton on the Hill. Here the picturesque stone houses line the road and their raised gardens have given the fanciful name of the Babylon of the Cotswolds to the village.

Near the top of the hill a turning to the right leads to Blockley along the side of Bourton wood. After about a mile there is a fine view of Blockley, below and in front. Blockley is a Cotswold village with a difference. Though as picturesque as any, it was the most industrialised of north Cotswold places. In the nineteenth century there were at least eight mills on the Blockley stream. Most were converted from corn-milling to silk-spinning mills and the village was the centre for this in the Cotswolds. It is difficult to believe this now as all the mills have been converted to residences or demolished, but at least one mill pool remains. The old houses are built on terraces up the hillside and make an attractive scene. The large church contains memorials to the Spencer-Churchill and Rushout families; the latter became Lord Northwick of Northwick Park. This great house is now apartments and a business centre lies on the edge of the park.

One of the pleasant features of Blockley is the path through Dovedale, a wooded valley to the south of the village. This is part of the Five Mile Drive, a carriage road from the gates of Northwick Park making a circular drive. Made probably in the 1820s, it is now largely, but not entirely, a public footpath or bridleway where it is not part of the main road.

We take the road leaving the village by its north-west corner towards Chipping Campden and, after passing the edge of Northwick Park, come to a spot where a memorial seat on the right gives a wide view over Broad Campden to Chipping Campden. Broad Campden is a tiny village which has several buildings of interest. The Norman Chapel House is to the left of the road behind a wall and topiary. This was restored as a private house by C. R. Ashbee, the leader of the Guild of Handicrafts, who we will meet again in Chipping Campden. The little nineteenth-century church is on a bank above the small green at the junction of several ways. The Quaker Meeting House, recorded as being in use in the latter half of the seventeenth century, is tucked away down a side lane here but this did not save it from being damaged by the religious intolerance of the time. It is interesting to note that a descendant of one of the families associated with its founding, William Warner of Blockley, emigrated to America and founded a settlement which is now part of Philadelphia.

The road goes downhill towards Chipping Campden and enters the town by Sheep Street. Chipping (market town) Campden is reputed to have the best houses in the north Cotswolds. Based on its prosperity from the wool trade in medieval times and added to by buildings in the following centuries, it was still a very suitable place to which the architect Charles Robert Ashbee transferred the workshops of his Guild of Handicrafts from London in 1902. About 150 people eventually moved. These craftsmen, inspired by the ideals of William Morris, worked mainly in wood and metal, to which printing was later added, to produce articles of better quality than the generally available factory produced ones. Unfortunately the project was not financially viable, and the workshops closed down after a few years. Some of the workers stayed and the guild was re-formed as the Campden Trust, which undertook much restoration work in the neighbourhood, partly financed by a wealthy American, Joseph Fels. Ashbee was joined by the similarly minded architect, Griggs. The tradition of crafts-manship, especially silver-smithing, still survives in Campden.

A delightful account of his journey to Campden from Cirencester with a donkey cart in 1907 is given in Norman Jewson's book *By Chance I Did Rove*, published in 1973. 'In those days,' he wrote, 'before motoring had opened up the country, Campden was as remote and self-contained a little town as could

Chipping Campden church and gatehouse.

be found, and except on market days, peace and quiet seemed to have become its permanent portion.' Later Jewson joined Gimson and the Barnsleys in their Art and Craft workshops at Sapperton, at the head of the Stroud valley. Today, in summer at least, Campden is crowded with people, cars and coaches. Few have time to appreciate its beauties fully, for to do so you must walk through the village from the church downwards, taking a side road to see the almshouses. The main street is entirely of stone or timber with no intrusive brick anywhere.

The church is a fine example of Perpendicular style, one of the great wool churches of the Cotswolds. It has many similarities to the church at Northleach and the same mason may have worked on both. In the chancel is a large brass of William Grevil, a wool merchant who died 1401, and his wife. He is reputed to have done much for the town and the church though it was not built until after his death. Preserved in a glass case are examples of Campden's greatest treasure, pre-Reformation altar needlework.

In the south transept, contrasting strongly with the architectural unity of the rest of the building, are the seventeenth-century tombs of the Hicks, Lord Campden's family. Sir Baptist Hicks who died in 1629, did much for the town and had a great house nearby. However it was destroyed in the Civil War to prevent it falling into the hands of the parliamentarians. All that remains of it are the gateway or lodge and an isolated building in a field, probably a summerhouse.

A little down from the lodge, and on the opposite side of the road, are the Hicks Almshouses, a plain eight-gabled terrace of early seventeenth-century Cotswold houses.

Near the top of the main street is the pointed archway which leads to the Ernest Wilson memorial garden. A son of Campden, he was a collector of plants

97

from China in the early years of the twentieth century and responsible for the introduction of many plants now well known in gardens. Eventually he became director of the Arnold Arboretum in the United States.

On the opposite side is Grevil's house with its Perpendicular style bay window, showing how that style came to be applied to houses as well as churches. There are many buildings of interest in this remarkable street, but it is probably best not to try and see them all individually but to absorb the scene as a whole. Only two others will be mentioned: the Woolstaplers' Hall, now a museum incorporating a fourteenth-century hall with oak-beamed roof, and the market hall in the middle of the street, another of Sir Baptist Hicks' contributions to the town.

Campden is a place to linger in, but our Cotswold drive continues by taking the western extension of the High Street towards Weston-sub-Edge which takes us to the National Trust car park at the top of Dover's Hill. This was the scene of Dover's, or the Cotswold, games, started in 1612 by Robert Dover. They were a popular annual event with country sports, like racing, wrestling, even shin-kicking, until they became too rowdy, it is said due to an influx of people from the Midlands, and were closed down in 1851. In recent years they have been revived as the Cotswold Olympick Games, held in Whitsun week.

Former Fish Inn, Fish Hill, Broadway.

A walk along the grassy bank on the top of the hill past the indicator gives a fine view of the vale towards Evesham.

We return to the road towards Broadway and follow it to meet the main road to Stow and Moreton, the A44, at the top of Fish Hill. Opposite, between tall stone posts, is the way to Broadway Tower and Country Park. The tower, a fine mock-Norman tower built about 1800, was used by the Guild of Handicrafts for a printing press, and examples of William Morris's work and designs are displayed there. The view from the top in clear weather extends from the Welsh mountains to the cooling towers of Didcot power station in the Thames Valley.

Between the present main road and the entrance to Fish Hill quarry are the remains of the old road. The quarry is a busy place for the quarrying and cutting of Cotswold stone. A little way along the old road is the now rather forlorn

Stanway House.

building, formerly the Fish Inn, once on the main road but now well above it. The building has some curious and incongruous architectural features.

We now return to the vale by going down the sweeping new road to Broadway. This village is perhaps the best known of all Cotswold villages, its broad street being world famous as an example of what is considered one of the most typical of English villages. The individual buildings do not have the quality and interest of those in Chipping Campden, but the houses of different dates blend together very well. This gives an air of distinction, especially so now that stricter car parking rules have reduced the number of cars left in the main street. A car park has been made behind the houses and shops.

This was not the original main part of the village. Once again it is an example of a village that has moved from around the old church to a new site. The old church of St Eadburga, dating from the twelfth century, is at Bury End and probably nearer the original way down the hill.

The present road to Cheltenham leaves the Evesham road and is the turnpike of the eighteenth century. It by-passes four villages three of which are characteristically Cotswold and are reached by side lanes. The first is Buckland, where the few houses line the road before it finishes at the manor close to the church. This has some original seventeenth-century woodwork and a very early pre-Reformation cope preserved in a glass case. The old rectory has a hall with a fine timber roof of the fifteenth century.

The next place of interest is Stanton with its many houses with their varied and complex roof lines. It is a nearly perfect small Cotswold stone village and owes much of its attractiveness to the work of Sir Phillip Stott, an architect, who bought the estate in 1906 and sensitively improved many of the houses. It is now a very favoured village for residence and is best explored on one of the days in summer when its gardens are open. At the highest point of the village is the Moat Inn. Up a separate drive above it is Stanton Guildhouse built in 1972 by volunteers as a centre where craft skills could be taught and where individual and community needs could be met.

From this end of the village also an old quarry road and holloway leads up the hill and a path goes to Shenberrow Camp on the top. This was partly excavated in 1935 when Iron Age objects were found.

From Stanton a lane leads to Stanway past the cricket ground which has all the characteristics expected of an English village cricket ground, green pitch, great trees, even a thatched pavilion supported on staddle stones.

On the other side of the road is the great park avenue of horse chestnuts leading to Stanway House. The range of yellow-stone buildings is seen across lawns and partly hidden by its trees and was built in Elizabethan and Stuart times. A conspicuous feature is the tall window at the end of the range which lights the great hall. In the grounds is a tithe barn with massive timbers supporting a Cotswold tile roof, made for the Abbey of Tewkesbury. At the top of the slope behind the house is the pyramid, a landmark from distant view-points, which was built at the top of a cascade which no longer exists. The most imposing building in the village however is the great ornamental gatehouse of about 1630 with both Renaissance and Tudor details in its yellow stone. The scallop shells on the gables are the emblem of the Tracy family who acquired the manor after the Dissolution.

From Stanway the lane reaches the Stow road at the war memorial, a fine bronze of St George and the dragon. The lane opposite goes through Didbrook which has two good examples of cruck-beam cottages, showing the great timber gable ends on which the roof ridge is supported. This is the village to which people from Hailes were moved when the abbey was built. The church was built for them by the abbot about 1475. It is one of the local churches which still has the seventeenth-century pulpit and communion rails and old timbered pews, and has been described in chapter seven.

From Didbrook past the turning to Hailes, it is only a short distance to Winchcombe and the completion of this drive which has tried to explore some of the most interesting places in the north Cotswolds.

Select Bibliography

Adlard, E., *A Short History of Postlip Mill* (F. Muller, 1950).

Adlard, E., *Winchcombe Cavalcade* (E. J. Burrow, 1939).

Aldred, D. H., *Cleeve Hill: The History of the Common and its People* (Alan Sutton Publishing, 1990).

Brill, E., *Life and Tradition in the Cotswolds* (Alan. Sutton Publishing, 1988).

Countryside Commission, *The Cotswold Landscape* (Countryside Commission, Cheltenham, 1990).

Daubeny, J. F., *Cleeve Common* (1900).

Dent, E., *Annals of Winchcombe and Sudeley* (1877).

Dreghorn, W., *Geology Explained in the Severn Vale and Cotswolds* (David and Charles, 1967).

English Place Names Society (A. H. Smith), *The Place Names of Gloucestershire*, Part 2 (Cambridge University Press, 1964).

Evans, H. A., *Highways and Byways in Oxfordshire and the Cotswolds* (1905).

Finberg, J., *Gloucestershire Studies* (Leicester University Press, 1957).

Fosbroke, T. D., *A Picturesque and Topographical Account of Cheltenham* (1826).

Garrett, J. H., *From a Cotswold Height* (1919; reprinted A. Sutton Publishing, 1988, 1992).

Gissing, A., *The Footpath Way in Gloucestershire* (1924).

Gloucestershire Trust for Nature Conservation, *Gloucestershire Commons: Their History, Wildlife and Future* (1989).

Grundy, G. B., *Saxon Charters and Field Names in Gloucestershire* (Bristol and Gloucestershire Archaeological Society, 1935–36).

Haigh, G., *The History of Winchcombe Abbey* (Skeffington, 1947).

Hencken, T. C., 'The Excavation of the Iron Age Camp on Bredon Hill', *Archaeol. Jnl.* 95, i. 1938.

Holland, S. C., *et al.*, *Supplement to the Flora of Gloucestershire* (Grenfell Publications, Bristol, 1986).

Mabey, R., *The Common Ground* (Hutchinson and Co., 1980).

Mellersh, W. L., *A Treatise on the Birds of Gloucestershire* (1902).

Pevsner, N., *The Buildings of England: Worcestershire* (1968).

Riddlesdell, H. J., *et al. Flora of Gloucestershire* (Chatford House Press, Bristol, 1948).

Richardson, L., *A Handbook to the Geology of Cheltenham* (1904).

Royal Commission on Historical Monuments, *Iron Age and Romano-British Monuments in the Gloucestershire Cotswolds* (HMSO, 1976).

Saville, A. (ed.), *Archaeology in Gloucestershire* (Cheltenham Art Gallery and Bristol and Gloucester Archaeological Society, 1984).

St Clair, Baddeley W. A., *Cotswold Shrine* (1908).

Swaine, C. M., *Birds of Gloucestershire* (Alan. Sutton Publishing, 1982).

Verey, *The Buildings of England: Gloucestershire*, vols 1 and 2 (1970).

Verey, D., *The Diary of a Cotswold Parson* (A. Sutton Publishing, 1979).

Victoria County History: Gloucestershire, vol viii (OUP, 1968).

Witchell, C. D. and Strugnell, W. B., *Fauna and Flora of Gloucestershire* (1892).

Index